Mend

or

Spend

How to Force Rich People to Solve Economic Inequality

Cody Cain

ISBN 978-0-578-46416-9

For all who believe
we can create a free and fair society.

Contents

Contents

Contents

Chapter

1

Summary Overview

Our beloved society has been turned upside down.

The wealthy 1% at the top dominate the rest of the 99% down below. This is wrong. It is time to solve the problem.

We must change the rules of the game. No more becoming rich by exploiting the common people. Those who possess the greatest strength must no longer be permitted to use their advantages to enrich themselves. Instead, the people at the top must be forced to improve the lives of those down below. Otherwise, they will not be permitted to remain rich.

The core of the problem is economic inequality. We must solve economic inequality in order to restore fairness in our society. We must create a more perfect union.

Fortunately, a simple solution exists.

Just have the rich people fix it.

After all, the rich people have all the money. If they would just share some of their wealth more fairly, then economic inequality would be solved.

Rich people also possess the expertise about how money is earned and distributed in the economy. So the rich are exactly the right people to work on this problem. They could devise improvements to our economic system to share wealth more equally among all classes of people instead of being overwhelmingly concentrated at the top.

Sounds terrific.

But there is one little wrinkle. How in the world could rich people be persuaded to work on this problem?

Rich people have no incentive whatsoever to fix the malfunction because they benefit from the existing system just the way it is, thank you. The existing system makes them rich. So they have no desire to work toward a solution that would make them less rich.

This conflict lies at the heart of the problem. And it is no small matter. In fact, it is an enormous issue. It exposes a deep defect that, much to our consternation, amounts to nothing less than a fatal flaw in our entire economic system.

Our society is structurally incapable of solving one of its greatest problems. Not only is our system unable to solve the dysfunction, but, in fact, it perpetuates the dysfunction. It perceives as threats any attempts to correct the malady and thus quashes them. Our very own beloved system has become part of the problem.

The best and the brightest people in our society, and those with the greatest advantages, rise to the top and become rich. Once at the top, rich people acquire a disproportionate amount of political power and thus largely control society. They use their power not to improve society for other people down below, but instead to protect their own wealth. They thwart any reforms that threaten to pry away a portion of their wealth in order to share it more equitably.

So the ablest and most powerful members of society not only have no desire or incentive to solve society's greatest problem, but in fact they have every incentive to actively prevent the problem from being solved.

This is backwards. Bungled. Dysfunctional. And wrong.

A society based upon a structure that prevents its own problems from being solved is a society that is broken.

But a solution exists to break through this breakdown.

The incentives must be changed. It is as simple as that. Currently, the wealthy are incentivized to block all solutions to economic inequality. So instead, the incentives must be reformed to induce the wealthy to solve economic inequality.

The proper incentive structure is easy to envision. The system must be corrected so that the wealthy would stand to gain financially by solving economic inequality, and would stand to lose financially while the problem remains unsolved. If these incentives were implemented, the wealthy would spring into action to solve the problem so fast our heads would spin. We would suddenly see a newfound spirit of egalitarianism materialize out of thin air.

The policy proposal for implementing these proper incentives is "Mend or Spend."

The concept is to present a clear and simple choice to the wealthy. On the one hand, the wealthy could choose voluntarily to "mend" the system. In this case, the wealthy would participate in a process to solve economic inequality by working with other stakeholders to develop and implement practical solutions.

On the other hand, if the wealthy failed to solve the problem voluntarily, then they would be forced to "spend" their own money. If economic inequality has not improved by a predetermined future deadline, then the wealthy would be forced to "spend" their money through the imposition of a steep income tax rate. The tax would apply only to the wealthy and not to anyone else. The revenue would be used to correct economic inequality by funding a multitude of public programs designed to benefit the middle class and the poor throughout society.

In essence, "Mend or Spend" starts a ticking clock on the wealthy. They will be given a set amount of time to voluntarily "mend" the system with new policies. But if they fail, they would then be forced to "spend" their own money on the problem through the imposition of a hearty tax.

At first blush, Mend or Spend might seem like a solution that resorts to "soaking the rich." But, in fact, the basis of Mend or Spend extends deeper. The magic of Mend or Spend is that it harnesses the power of the free market and, with one simple stroke, mobilizes the entire marketplace by introducing a strong incentive to solve economic inequality.

It is a market-based solution. There is no need to resort to socialism or communism. Capitalism remains in-tact. It is just a fairer form of capitalism. It reflects a more equitable system of "balanced capitalism."

Mend or Spend. It's up to the wealthy to choose their preference. Clear and simple. Yet extraordinarily powerful.

Could a solution like this actually be passed into law?

Absolutely!

The wealthy, of course, would first wage an extraordinary battle to prevent it from ever taking effect. But despite their might, the wealthy can be overcome. When the great masses of the population unite, we will prevail.

A key aspect of Mend or Spend is that it is genuinely non-partisan. It equally benefits both the political right and left. It cuts through identity politics to appeal to all races, genders, and religions. It unites everyone in the 99%. Those are good odds.

Economic inequality can be solved. The masses of the powerless can join together and compel the powerful to share their wealth. Society can be improved by becoming more fair and enjoyable for the great majority of its citizens.

Mend or Spend is the solution.

Now, it is up to us – We the People – to make it happen. Incredibly, the miracle of democracy has given us the power to determine our own fate. And the solution is remarkably easy to achieve. All it takes is a vote.

Our future is in our own hands.

Chapter

2

Trouble in Paradise: Economic Inequality

America is known around the world as "the land of opportunity." And indeed this is how we think of ourselves. As the old adage goes, anyone can get ahead by simply working hard and playing by the rules. Now that sounds like a fair deal.

But, alas, for this deal has been pulled out from under us. It has become a one-sided deception. After we fulfill our end of the bargain by working hard and playing by the rules, we are denied the opportunity to get ahead.

Something has gone awry.

2.1 Pyramid of Inequality

When we consider the big picture of our society, we see a very troubling system. The structure of our society has shaped itself into an unfair pyramid. Sitting at the top of the pyramid are a very small number of people who are extremely wealthy and powerful, the so-called 1%. The rest of the people, the 99%, make-up the remaining portion of the middle and base of the pyramid. The very few rich and powerful at the top of the pyramid rule over the rest of the people down below.

Instead of the wealth of our society being shared more fairly to provide the people with living wages and decent lives, the people are left with only small sums to scrape by and keep them working for the next paycheck while much of the wealth is sucked up to the top of the pyramid where the wealthy few enjoy lavish riches for themselves.

It is a crazy system. The distribution of rewards does not correspond to the amount of benefit being contributed to society. The people at the top of the pyramid, primarily investors and corporate executives, earn tens of millions of dollars for themselves while ordinary citizens down below cannot afford basic essentials, like affordable housing, healthcare, safe communities, education, childcare, elderly care, healthy food, and on and on. Great fortunes can be made by gaming the system, exploiting others, delivering large audiences with mindless content, harming our society, or spinning the wheel of fortune, but it is much more difficult to make money by actually helping real human beings or improving our society.

This is not the nation it once was. This is not the nation we desire it to be.

Our society is unfair. It is plagued with the scourge of drastic economic inequality.

2.2   We Are Not Asking for Much

We the people do not need very much to be satisfied.

Need, not greed, is the source of our discontent.

The goal is not to make everyone rich or to impose exact equality among every individual. We are not seeking extreme measures like a government take-over of the means of production, abolishing private ownership of property, or anything of the kind. The idea is not to create some sort of bizarre society where everyone is forced to be identical to everyone else and all citizens must wear the exact same clothes, live in the exact same houses, and own the exact same belongings. This, of course, would be absurd.

All we seek is that every citizen must be financially secure. That's it. Financial security. Clear and simple. That's all we need.

Today, people are forced to live under the constant threat of financial insecurity. We are always worried about how we can support ourselves and our families. Many jobs do not pay sufficient wages to meet our basic needs. And even people lucky enough to have a decent job are still not safe. We live under the enormous stress of always knowing that we are no more than one small step away from financial ruin. A single mishap would wreck our lives, such as losing a job, having an accident, or a family member falling ill.

We live under a financial sword of Damocles always dangling precariously above us knowing full well that it could fall at any moment. This subjects us to the strain of constant anxiety. It forces us into jobs we despise and drives us to toil away for long hours at insufficient wages.

We are deprived of free time. We are denied self-fulfillment. We are barred from the pursuit of happiness.

We experience a sense of dissatisfaction with our lives. We do not understand why we are angry at our loved ones and at the world. We feel humiliated, debased, and disrespected.

We are robbed of nothing less than our own lives as free human beings.

It is not difficult to imagine what it would take to alleviate this condition. An abundance of agreeable jobs would work wonders, either in the private sector or in government. These jobs would be readily available, would not be overly demanding, would not require long hours, and would pay wages that provided a comfortable living.

Just imagine if one could easily take a job as, say, a teacher, a care-provider to the elderly, or in a park, for a few days a week and earn a good living, including healthcare, child care, and a sufficient retirement. If decent jobs were always available, then no one would ever need to worry about how to support themselves and their families.

People would also not be forced to endure miserable conditions in other jobs, because they could always just quit those jobs knowing that they could easily take a different job. This, of course, would lead to improved working conditions throughout the marketplace because all employers, private and public, would be forced to provide pleasant conditions in order to attract workers.

Worker participation in the economy would increase because jobs would be abundant and much more enjoyable. And for those unable to work, society would provide resources to ensure that people would not be abandoned.

Financial security. That's all it takes.

Isn't this the society we all desire?

So why don't we have it?

Is it impossible? Is it too much to ask?

No! It's not too much to ask. This is exactly the society we should have.

But it is not the society that exists today.

2.3   Age Old Unfairness

The issue of economic inequality has been around for ages. It is nothing new. It is not a contemporary problem that has grown out of our complex modern era. No. Economic inequality has existed for millennia. Literally.

Both Plato and Aristotle wrote about economic inequality way back in ancient Athens, Greece, the cradle of democracy, around the year 400 B.C., some 2,400 years ago. These two philosophers are widely considered to be nothing less than the fathers of Western thought. Plato was a student of Socrates, and Aristotle a student of Plato.

Plato's book, the "Republic," and Aristotle's book, "Politics," are seminal works that ponder the essential question of how best to establish the ideal society, and then they set about to provide the answer. These crucial works continue to serve as the foundation of Western governments of today. In these books, both men seek to set forth the best possible form of government for humankind. When the Founding Fathers of America were creating the American system of government, they drew heavily from these works for guidance.

In contemplating the ideal society, Plato and Aristotle both recognize that the distribution of wealth among the population is a central issue that must be addressed and properly managed. Both Plato and Aristotle identify economic inequality as a critical issue that will confront every society. Rich people and poor people are sure to emerge, and the crucial question is what to do about this situation.

Both men conclude that excessive economic inequality is so dangerous that it must be prevented. Otherwise, economic inequality will tear apart the fabric of society and lead to its destruction.

Economic inequality to them is no joke. It is an existential threat.

2.3.1   Plato

Plato contends that economic inequality will become worse and worse. And he lays the blame at the feet of the wealthy. As the rich "grow richer and richer," he writes, "the more they think of making a fortune the less they think of virtue."

Astounding words.

The cause of economic inequality was plainly identified over two thousand years ago.

According to Plato, this increasing inequality leads to such great division within society that two separate factions form within the state: the rich and the poor. These two groups become so diametrically opposed that eventually they go to war against one another and destroy the state.

To prevent extreme economic inequality from developing, Plato believes that the wealthy must not be permitted to rule society. Instead, the rulers of society must remain strictly independent from wealthy interests. Otherwise, if the rulers themselves were tied to financial interests, they would become compromised and could not act fairly. The rulers would make laws that favored the wealthy and disfavored the poor. This would exacerbate economic inequality and lead to great unfairness throughout society.

To ensure that the rulers were financially independent, the rulers would be prohibited from owning property themselves. Instead, they would earn their living through a modest public salary. This way, the rulers would be financially secure while remaining free from undue influence by either the rich or the poor, and thus they would enact fair laws for the good of everyone equally and for the benefit of society overall.

To cultivate these rulers, society would groom and train its most exceptional youth in order to prepare them for future leadership. The system is based upon individual merit thereby permitting candidates to emerge from the common people. They would be selected based upon their superior intellectual abilities as well as their strength of moral character. They would be given the finest educations, taught to maintain their independence from the corrupting influence of the wealthy, and trained to make virtuous decisions based upon the good of society overall.

Not bad.

America, of course, did not follow these recommendations. Today, Plato would be appalled by the extent to which American politicians are so closely tied to wealthy corporations. This corrupts politicians by causing them to enact laws that favor the wealthy and hinder everyone else. Plato would denounce our American republic for destroying the independence of politicians, favoring the wealthy over the middle class and the poor, causing drastic economic inequality, and ultimately threatening the existence of the republic itself.

2.3.2   Aristotle

Aristotle agrees with Plato that economic inequality poses a grave threat to society. Aristotle's approach to solving the problem is based in the notion of economic classes.

Aristotle, ever the realist, accepts that societies will inevitably consist of some level of economic inequality. There will be a rich class and a poor class. This alone is not fatal so long as the disparity is not excessive. For Aristotle, the answer lies in maintaining an acceptable balance between the rich and the poor.

Aristotle's concern is that both the rich and the poor are at opposite extremes in conflict with each other, and if either becomes too large, then the balance will be upset and chaos will ensue.

The risk of upsetting the balance essentially lies with the rich. They are too greedy. As Aristotle remarks, "the encroachments of the rich are more destructive to the [state] than those of the people."

Stunning words.

Over two thousand years ago, it was clearly recognized that the wealthy at the top are responsible for creating economic inequality in society.

According to Aristotle, the rich continuously seek to increase their wealth at the expense of the middle class and the poor. As the rich take away greater and greater amounts from the middle class, more and more people fall out of the middle class and into the ranks of the poor. This erodes the middle class and increases the extremes on both ends as the rich become richer and the poor become larger and larger in number.

If the poor become too many, troubles arise. If the poor become an overwhelming majority, they could use their democratic powers to enact laws that confiscate the property of the wealthy and redistribute it to the poor. Or worse, the poor could revolt. They could rise up, march against the rich, kill them, and take all their property to redistribute it among themselves. In either case, the state will come to an end.

The key for Aristotle is that society must always maintain a sufficiently large and healthy middle class. The middle class is the glue that holds together the entire state. The people in the middle class are not rich enough to be overcome with avarice and thus they do not seek to oppress the poor below them. They are also not rich enough for the poor to resent them. And the middle class are not poor enough to rise up and march against the rich.

Instead, the people of the middle class are perfectly content with their own situation and thus they are satisfied with the state. They stand in between the rich and the poor and balance the entire system. They work hard, they play by the rules, and they enjoy their lives. They have no reason to oppose the state.

Thus a large and robust middle class is the essential element in keeping the society in balance and ensuring the continuation of the state.

In effect, this puts the onus on the rich. They must restrain their own impulses toward greed in order to maintain a large middle class and limit the size of the poor class. Otherwise, if the rich extract too much for themselves, they will upset the balance and cause the destruction of society, including their own demise.

If Aristotle were here today, he would denounce the situation in America. He would warn that the system is out of balance. The rich are too rich. They are failing to restrain their own greed. Instead, the rich are relentlessly plundering the middle class by suppressing wages, slashing benefits, and shipping jobs overseas under globalization. More and more people are being pushed out of the middle class and into the ranks of the poor while the rich grow ever richer.

Aristotle would warn that these are telltale signs indicating that America is careening down the path toward catastrophe.

2.3.3   The French Revolution

Plato and Aristotle offered pearls of wisdom about the dangers posed by economic inequality. But, alas, for posterity failed to heed their warnings. Some two thousand years later, many governments around the world had formed themselves into oppressive monarchies and empires based upon economic inequality.

The warnings of the philosophers, however, were about to be exhumed to echo resoundingly through the ages.

In 1789, the French Revolution changed the world forever. The class of poor peasants had finally had enough of economic inequality. They took up arms, marched on Paris, and stormed the Bastille, a government building and prison. The peasants overthrew the monarchy, beheaded King Louis XVI and Queen Marie Antoinette, and installed themselves as the new rulers of France.

This revolution sent shockwaves throughout Europe and around the world.

Unfortunately, the overthrow by the peasants did not produce peace and harmony. Instead, it ignited an era of chaos and violence that lasted for decades.

Within France, the peasants failed to govern the country effectively and instead became oppressors themselves. They began with good intentions. They desired to create a virtuous society. This was wonderful, especially after such tyrannical rule by monarchs.

But once in power, the peasants proved to be awful rulers themselves. They grew increasingly intolerant of criticism and anyone with opposing views. Large numbers of dissidents and protestors were soon being unfairly jailed and executed. The rule of the peasants was so egregious and violent that it became known as the "Reign of Terror."

The peasants as rulers turned out to be just as bad if not worse than the monarchs. As a result, French society suffered from severe internal conflict.

Externally, the revolution plunged France into the French Revolutionary Wars (1792-1802) against various European powers. A consequence of the French Revolution was that France's European neighbors were incentivized to wage war against France. Some of the other monarchies in Europe felt threatened by the peasant overthrow and desired to restore a monarchy in France to prevent this revolutionary fervor from spreading into their own countries. And some European powers saw an opportunity. With France weakened by their internal revolution, these powers could attack France and seize French territory for themselves.

After a decade of internal strife and external wars, the French people grew so disaffected that this led to the rise of the military commander Napoleon Bonaparte as the leader of France in 1799, ending the French Revolution.

Napoleon was essentially a dictator. In 1804, he crowned himself Emperor of France. This effectively returned France to the very form of authoritarian rule that the revolution had sought to overthrow in the first place.

Authoritarian rule, of course, was not the answer. The ascension of Napoleon led to another decade of war under the Napoleonic Wars (1803-1815) of France against the European powers caused by the unresolved tensions from the prior French Revolutionary Wars.

Napoleon was eventually defeated at the Battle of Waterloo in present day Belgium in 1815, deposed from power, banished from France, and exiled to the remote island of Saint Helena in the middle of the South Atlantic Ocean over a thousand miles from the west coast of Africa where he died in isolation in 1821.

By this time, France and Europe had endured the horror of over 25 years of war since the beginning of the French Revolution in 1789.

In the aftermath of the revolution, numerous monarchies in Europe and elsewhere around the world had fallen or were forced to concede aspects of their power.

Indeed, the consequences of economic inequality can be profound.

2.3.4   Revolutionary Highlights Tour

While the French Revolution serves as perhaps the marquee example of class revolution, it is by no means the only example. History is rife with incidents in which economic inequality was a factor in cataclysmic social upheavals. Let us briefly touch upon but a few.

<u>Roman Empire</u>. Long before the French Revolution, economic inequality played a role in nothing less than the decline and fall of the Roman Empire.

Rome existed for about one thousand years from approximately 500 B.C.E. to 500 C.E. As the empire expanded, subjects from conquered territories were increasingly sent back to Rome as slaves. The wealthy aristocrats exploited this newfound source of cheap labor, which depressed the wages of Roman workers. The aristocrats also acquired ever more land from middle class farmers. So the common people lost their jobs and their land. They were being squeezed out of the middle class and into the ranks of the poor, all while ever more wealth was being concentrated into the hands of the upper class.

This is strikingly similar to the situation in America today. Under globalization, the wealthy elite are exporting middle class jobs overseas. This is the equivalent to the Romans importing slaves. In both cases, the middle class workers lose their jobs to cheap foreign labor.

And just like the Roman elite increased their wealth and power by consolidating more and more land, the American elite today are increasing their wealth and power by consolidating larger and larger corporations.

In times of economic hardship, the suffering masses often turn to populist leaders in the desperate hope of electing a savior.

The military general Julius Caesar rose to power in 49 B.C.E. in part by recognizing the affliction of economic inequality. He gained tremendous popularity with the lower classes by appealing to their unfair economic condition and promising reforms to reverse economic inequality.

As with many populist leaders, however, Julius Caesar also harbored a lust for personal power. He undermined democratic institutions and seized ever more control of the Roman government, ultimately declaring himself dictator for life.

His usurpation of power proved to be his downfall. The Roman senate became alarmed by his autocratic actions. On the Ides of March (the 15th day of March), in the year 44 B.C.E., during a session of the senate, conspiring senators stepped forth, drew their daggers, and famously assassinated Julius Caesar.

His removal, however, did not restore democracy to Rome. It was too late. Democracy had been lost.

Julius Caesar had transformed Rome away from the great Roman "Republic" governed democratically with participation by the people, and into the Roman "Empire" ruled forever after by emperors.

Rome eventually became plagued with internal conflicts. Drastic economic inequality persisted. Politics became increasingly divisive and extreme. Political candidates developed their own loyal constituencies by promoting allegiance to the candidate instead of to Rome. The candidates even assembled their own armies loyal to the candidate instead of to the state. This fostered factions and extreme polarization within Roman society. Political successions were repeatedly determined not by debates between the candidates, but instead by civil wars between the candidates.

Rome was tearing itself apart from within. Drastic economic inequality contributed to the extreme division in society. The Roman Empire, that had once been the great Roman Republic, began a gradual decline that lasted for hundreds of years until it eventually collapsed forever in 476 C.E.

Haitian Revolution (1791).   The consequences of the French Revolution of 1789 rippled around the globe. One significant consequence occurred in the Caribbean nation of Haiti. France had colonized Haiti in the mid 1600s, subjugated the indigenous population, imported African slaves, imposed a brutal form of slavery, and, in the middle decades of the 1700s, began mass producing sugar as a highly profitable commodity for trade on international markets.

Upon learning of the French Revolution, the slaves in Haiti dared to presume that they also were included in the "Declaration of the Rights of Man" issued in connection with the French Revolution that proclaimed universal freedom for all human beings. The French colonists in Haiti, however, did not quite share this enlightened perspective and violently cracked down on any such subversive inclinations.

In 1791, the black slaves revolted, led by the charismatic former slave, Toussaint L'Ouverture. The slaves violently overthrew their white plantation masters, defeated the European armies in battle, and, in 1804, established their own free and independent nation of Haiti.

It was the first successful slave uprising throughout the colonial world, and it sent shockwaves through the white European nations. It was the only slave revolt that gave rise to a new nation governed by non-whites and former enslaved people.

Latin American Wars of Independence (1800s). The Spanish Empire was rocked to its core as well. The French Revolution of 1789 had given rise to the Napoleonic Wars, which resulted in Napoleon conquering Spain in 1808.

At this point in time, Spain had amassed an enormous empire in Latin America. After Christopher Columbus had historically crossed the Atlantic Ocean for Spain in 1492 seeking a new trade route to China and India but instead accidentally "discovering" America, Spain colonized almost the entire new world of Latin America. Spain colonized Mexico, Central America, and South America, with the main exception of Brazil, which was colonized by Portugal.

So three centuries later when the overlord country of Spain was vexed by the invasion of Napoleon – the Spanish invader had itself been invaded – all of a sudden, the collection of Latin American countries recognized an opportunity to break free from Spanish colonial oppression.

And this is precisely what they did. They made a run for it.

In an extraordinary burst of upheavals during only a short period of the early decades in the 1800s, virtually every country in Latin America broke away from Spanish rule. One country after the next. Truly astonishing.

Brazil also broke free as Napoleon had invaded Brazil's colonial overlord, Portugal, in 1807.

Nearly all of the countries that exist today in Latin America were formed at this time, from the southern tip of Argentina all the way up through the northern border of Mexico, including such countries as Colombia, Venezuela, Peru, Chile, Brazil, Mexico, and others.

When the peasants in France first took up arms against their monarchs and stormed the Bastille, little did they know that they were destined to set free Latin America.

European Revolutions of 1848. The Industrial Revolution of the early to mid decades of the 1800s, along with its corollary of brutal capitalism, caused tremendous disruptions across Western Europe, including substantial unemployment and stark economic inequality. The economic imbalance was in part responsible for triggering a wave of revolutions in 1848 that arose in numerous countries across Europe.

The rebels were primarily the working class who were seeking relief from economic oppression as well as greater democratic rights, increased participation in government, freedom of the press, and the relinquishment of power by monarchies. The revolutions began in France and spread to many countries, such as Germany, Italy, Switzerland, Denmark, the Netherlands, and others.

Economic unfairness can indeed cause the masses of the population to unite and take action.

Russian Revolution (1917). The Industrial Revolution spread to Russia around the turn of the twentieth century, and along with it came its signature features of disruption, unemployment, and economic inequality. Russia's involvement in World War I (1914-1918) exacerbated the hardships imposed upon its people, including food shortages.

The suffering workers took to the streets and, in 1917, overthrew their monarch Czar Nicholas II, thereby ending over three hundred years of the Romanov Dynasty and many centuries of imperial rule. Under the Bolshevik Party leader, Vladimir Lenin, the workers united together and established the world's first communist state of the Soviet Union.

Indeed, economic inequality has consequences.

Spanish Civil War (1936). In America today, we should all be shocked by the horrors that befell Spain in the twentieth century. This experience should serve as a cautionary tale and a bright red flashing warning alarm light that even modern societies, like our own, can suddenly spiral out of control into a nightmare scenario of barbaric violence, destruction, and atrocity.

In the early decades of the 1900s, Spain was a modern European nation. It had a rich history of having been one of the greatest empires the world had ever known. Yet it had become an empire in decline and was struggling to find its way forward.

For decades, the ultra-conservative monarchy was striving to retain its power while a growing democratic movement was seeking to abolish the monarchy and establish a form of government by the people. In 1931, King Alfonso XIII relented to public pressure, stepped down from the thrown, and enabled the establishment of a new republic. Elections were held and moderate liberals won a decisive majority in the new government.

The worldwide Great Depression of 1929 exacerbated economic inequality within Spain. The question of how to confront the hardship contributed to a severe political divide between conservatives on the right and liberals on the left. This is very similar to the increasing political divide today in America between Republicans on the right and Democrats on the left, exacerbated by the Financial Crisis of 2008.

In Spain, the divisiveness grew and grew and grew until it became so inflamed that the two political parties actually took up arms against each other and ignited a hideous civil war.

Unlike the American Civil War (1861-1865) where a clear front line existed between north and south, in Spain, the division was interwoven throughout the fabric of society. Conservatives against liberals. In every city, in every town. Conservative neighbor against liberal neighbor. Conservative father against liberal son. Conservative sibling against liberal sibling.

It was essentially a class conflict of the liberal working class against the conservative ruling monarchy. (Disturbingly, the opposing interests are strikingly similar to the Democratic and Republican parties in America today.) The liberal-left had the support of a majority of the population, including the workers, as well as elements of socialists, anarchists, and communists. The conservative-right consisted of monarchists, the wealthy class, and the dominant religion in society of the Catholic Church. Despite being in the minority, the conservative-right was determined to maintain power.

The trouble began in 1936 when a faction in the Spanish military favoring the conservative-right minority announced a *coup d'etat* to overthrow the majority liberal-left government that had been democratically elected. The military general, Francisco Franco, led the conservative-right segment of the military.

Just as society was divided politically between right and left, so too was the military. About half of the military sided with the conservative-right and the other half with the liberal-left. This dangerous division within the military illustrates the importance of the general principle of always keeping the military strictly non-partisan.

Franco and his conservative-right faction in the army launched a military attack inside their own country of Spain. It boggles the mind to imagine, but an actual shooting war broke out in this modern nation between conservatives and liberals with the nation's military taking part and fighting against itself. Franco even ordered aerial bombings of modern Spanish cities populated primarily by liberals.

The war was disastrous for the people of Spain. The destruction was unthinkable. Atrocities and political executions occurred on both sides. The death, misery, and human suffering were horrendous.

Franco and the minority conservative-right prevailed in the war in 1939. Franco installed himself as the dictator of Spain and immediately set about to consolidate his grip on power. He instituted a vicious campaign of retribution and purges to rid Spain of the liberal-left, including the murder of tens of thousands of dissidents, as well as countless victims of torture, disappearances, and mass deportations.

As dictator, Franco ruled Spain with an iron fist for almost four decades all the way up through 1975. He established a network of concentration camps where he sent hundreds of thousands of suspected liberals, some of whom were executed. And he imposed a set of repressive laws and measures aimed at crushing political opposition, such as banning political parties, prohibiting political associations, censoring the press, restricting cultural activities, establishing the Catholic Church as the official state religion, outlawing the use of regional languages, purging liberals from government and universities, militarizing the police, infiltrating civil society with a secret police force, and on and on.

This forty-year period of repression in Spain's history should serve as a wake-up call to Republicans and Democrats in America today. Even in the face of difficult economic challenges, a society must not allow itself to degenerate into extreme political polarization. The worst outcome of barbaric violence can quickly erupt even in a modern society like our own.

In light of all of these devastating rebellions throughout the ages, it turns out that Plato and Aristotle were rather astute about the dangers posed by economic inequality.

2.3.5   Magical Disappearing Act

It is rather curious that, in the modern times of today, maintaining economic fairness is not regarded as an important objective for our own society.

Despite the fact that both Plato and Aristotle emphasized the critical importance of maintaining economic fairness in order to preserve the health of a society, and despite the horrendous consequences laid bare before the world of the French Revolution and many other rebellions, somehow this issue has been erased from our ideals today.

Financial equality is not a principle revered by modern society. We hear about economic inequality only in reports about its recent onset. But we have not established economic fairness as an ideal that we should strive to achieve. We do not teach school children that economic fairness is important to the health of society. We do not illuminate the dynamics of class structure and the dangers of class imbalances. Our government has no agencies or senior officials dedicated to maintaining economic balance within society. Our economic system rewards those who exploit the masses but not those who seek to provide for the less fortunate.

If anything, our recent culture has spurned the classical teachings of financial fairness in favor of celebrating the pursuit of wealth, almost always in superficial and disingenuous portrayals. Popular culture commonly reflects this, such as in television shows like "Lifestyles of the Rich and Famous," "The Simple Life" with Paris Hilton, and "Keeping Up with the Kardashians." Our culture has adopted the "greed is good" credo personified by the character Gordon Gekko in the 1987 movie, "Wall Street."

Plato and Aristotle would be horrified to see a society inciting a frenzy of the pursuit of wealth at the expense of fostering economic fairness and balance throughout society. Indeed, Plato and Aristotle were no fans of the rich. They viewed the rich as the source of all sorts of menacing problems severely damaging to society as a whole. They viewed the rich as having a corrupting influence because the rich tended to act in their own self-interest to enhance their own wealth instead of acting for the benefit of others and for society overall. The corrupting influence of the rich must therefore be contained in order to preserve the health of the state.

Our modern-day society instead views the rich as dignified, important, and deserving of respect. We celebrate the rich as superstars and lionize them as heroes. This notion seems to be a perverted outgrowth of an over-passionate worship of free markets under laissez-faire capitalism.

According to this rationale, if someone is generating great profits, then they certainly must be contributing an abundance of benefits to society. Many consumers are buying their products, and therefore these products necessarily must be improving the lives of the population and benefitting the whole. It is a win-win situation for everyone. How wonderful.

But we should know better by now. Just think of the "robber barons" of the late 1800s and early 1900s during the Gilded Age, like Rockefeller, Carnegie, Mellon, Morgan, and Vanderbilt. They too were becoming extremely rich, and many citizens were benefitting from their products, such as oil, steel, and the railroads as the nation expanded during the Industrial Age.

But we know full well today that these robber barons were also engaging in horrendous business practices that exploited the middle class, the poor, and society overall. They inflicted terrible treatment upon their own workers and corrupted the public government, all to line their own pockets with ever more riches at the expense of everyone else.

This is captured by the wonderful term, "Gilded Age." It conjures an impression of extreme wealth by implying that everything gleamed with gold. But upon reflection, the term also connotes a deeper and more insightful meaning.

The term invites comparison to the contrasting term of a "golden age." A superficial "gilded" age falls far short of a superior "golden" age. After all, a golden item is solid gold throughout, whereas a gilded item is merely coated with a thin layer of gold applied only upon its surface. Lying hidden beneath the gilding is a cheaper material like wood or a common metal.

The term "Gilded Age" implies that the wealth in society was merely a thin layer on the surface representing only a rich few at the top, and that this wealth concealed a vast amount of poverty and suffering of the masses underneath.

The term was coined from the 1873 novel, "The Gilded Age," by the celebrated American author Mark Twain (and co-author Charles Dudley Warner) that satirized the greed and corruption of the wealthy elite at the time.

We should have learned from the example of the robber barons that rich people are not necessarily good and virtuous for society, but often, in fact, are ruthless and ruinous.

The greed and corruption of the robber barons of the Gilded Age were exactly the sort of destructive behaviors by the wealthy that Plato and Aristotle had recognized over two thousand years earlier. Yet somehow in our modern day this concern seems to have mysteriously vanished.

2.4　　Current Unfairness

We think of ourselves today as being so much more advanced than the societies of the past. And in many ways we are more advanced. After all, we have the internet, smart phones, and self-driving cars. Our democratic form of government is certainly a vast improvement over the tyranny of kings and dictators.

But in some ways, we have not advanced as much as we believe.

When it comes to the matter of economic inequality, shockingly, we remain trapped in the past.

The extent of wealth inequality in our own society is absolutely appalling.

The three richest Americans, Bill Gates, Warren Buffett, and Jeff Bezos, own more wealth than half of the entire population combined. Three individuals!

One single family, the Walton family, the owners of the Walmart retail chain, own more than 42% of the population.

The richest 1% of Americans own more wealth than the entire bottom 90%. By far. Almost twice as much more. The top 20% own 90% of all the wealth in the nation. The bottom 80% combined own only 10% of the wealth. A full 20% of the population own nothing at all.

Chief executive officers of corporations earn around 350 times as much as their average worker. This is up from only 20 times just a few decades ago.

The situation is similar globally. The richest 1% own more than half of all the world's wealth. The bottom 70% own only 2.7%.

When we compare our modern society to societies of the past, we realize that, when it comes to economic inequality, many similarities persist. This can be shocking to us today because we think of the old kingdoms as being drastically unfair, while at the same time believing that our own society is very fair. But the statistics tell a different story. It turns out that our society is very unfair much like the monarchies of old with 1% of the population being super-rich and the rest of the 99% left to struggle just to get by.

2.5   No, the Rich Don't Deserve So Much

Some say that our society is different from past unfair societies because the super-rich of today earned their wealth fair-and-square and thus deserve every penny.

This, of course, is exactly what the super-rich would like us all to believe. But c'mon. Are we really going to keep falling for that?

This sort of argument is exactly what the commoners fell for in the past. They were told that the king deserved to be much richer than all the rest because God selected the king and it was therefore God's will for the king to be this rich, and for you to be that poor. Well okay then. If this is God's wish then it must be right. And the people fell for it!

Today, we know this is nonsense. Yet in our own society, we fall for similar arguments that are equally as implausible, like that the super-rich earned their wealth by simply working harder.

Seriously? This makes no sense! Each day contains only 24 hours. Rich people could not possibly have worked that much harder than the great masses of citizens who work long hours day-in and day-out.

In fact, many of the super-rich do not even work at all. They lounge around all day in their mansions and golf clubs. The source of their income is not from their own work but from the work performed by others. Their income is from the annual profits generated from their investments and from the corporations they own. They are not exactly working harder when they never lift so much as a pinky.

We now know that becoming rich is not as simple as merely "working hard" and "playing by the rules." Just about everyone is willing to do that. Yet only a very small number of people ever become rich. Many other factors are involved.

One enormous factor is pure dumb luck. Show me a rich man and I'll show you the luck that made him. The factor of luck is often an advantage of birth, such as being born into wealth, having a high level of intelligence, or possessing some sort of surpassing talent. Or perhaps just being at the right place at the right time. Luck is a critical factor in success that is constantly overlooked.

Also, just because an enterprise is successful does not mean that it is entirely beneficial to society. Corporate endeavors often come with costs. Even though they generate wealth, they often create harmful effects as well. The robber barons of the Gilded Age are a prime example. While the Industrial Revolution created enormous wealth, it also created enormous suffering with widespread labor exploitation, destruction of existing enterprises, unemployment, environmental devastation, pollution, and on and on. Corporate mergers create wealth but often result in job losses. Achieving greater "efficiency," or productivity, such as with standardized assembly lines, can create greater profits, but often renders the work experience monotonous, dehumanizing, and unfulfilling.

Regardless of the reasons that give rise to a wealthy class, the enormous disparity in wealth in our society is simply too extreme to justify. Even if some people work harder or are smarter than others, fairness in a society is not achieved when only a tiny fraction of the population possesses an enormous amount of wealth while the vast majority of the population is left to suffer with shortages.

A fair society must provide adequately for all of its citizens.

Chapter

3

The Culprit: Capitalism

Economic inequality is not something that exists organically in nature. It is not like sunflowers, pine trees, or butterflies. It is not produced by the natural environment.

Economic inequality does not happen all by itself. It does not pop-out of nowhere. It does not just spontaneously come into existence.

Economic inequality is not imposed upon us by some mysterious phenomenon. It is not like lightning, earthquakes, or floods that are inflicted upon us by forces far beyond our control. It is not some sort of naturally occurring wonder.

No. Economic inequality is entirely created by humans. It is our own little invention.

It all relates to money and economics. These are man-made. Human beings make all the decisions about these matters, including all the decisions about the distribution of money within society. When the distribution is unequal, this means that certain people are affirmatively making the decision to give more money to some people and less money to other people.

Economic inequality exists because human beings created it and human beings are perpetuating it.

3.1   The "C" Word

What is the cause of our unfair economic inequality?

Simple: Capitalism.

What?! Capitalism? No! It cannot be!

Drilled into our heads is the belief that capitalism is wonderful. Capitalism delivers everything we cherish about America. Capitalism has given us the gifts of opportunity, choice, and wealth.

Plus, we are told, the only alternative to capitalism is socialism and communism, like in Russia and China, where the government oppresses the people, crushes political dissent, strips away personal freedom, censors the internet, arrests people for self-expression, and controls the economy like a criminal cartel, causing empty shelves in stores and dead-end jobs where no one can get ahead without corruption.

Horrors!

You wouldn't want that, now, would you?

No! America must not become Russia or China!

No! We want Capitalism!

And for good measure, criticism of capitalism must be forbidden. Ban the books!

Hm. It seems we have touched a nerve here.

It is rather astonishing that in this modern day and age, decades after the end of the Cold War, any criticism of capitalism, no matter how slight, still triggers hysterical reactions.

The truth, of course, is that no one desires to become Russia or China. These are totalitarian regimes ruled by tyrants. They are hardly examples of nations to emulate. We are not seeking to make our nation *worse*, we are seeking to make our nation *better*.

Indeed, beware of claims that our only alternative is to become Russia or China. Or that any changes to our society would destroy America by imposing some sort of extreme form of socialism. This is all pure nonsense.

And it is often propagated by none other than the rich themselves. The reason is perfectly understandable. The rich desire to frighten the population away from any thoughts about how to improve our system. Naturally. The rich know full well that any improvements to our society would likely reduce their own wealth and power.

But we must not allow ourselves to be manipulated by the rich.

A free society like our own must be able to openly criticize itself. This is the only way to identify and correct problems in order to preserve and improve our society. Self-assessment and constructive criticism are healthy and should be practiced continuously as a matter of ongoing maintenance of our democracy.

Criticizing our own system does not mean we hate America and are seeking to convert it into Russia or China. In fact, the exact opposite is the case. The fastest way to turn America into Russia or China is to suppress criticism.

So let us not be afraid to apply an honest assessment to our own system of capitalism.

3.2   A Blessing and a Curse

Our system of capitalism has many benefits. Perhaps the most striking feature is that capitalism is an enormously powerful system for motivating human endeavor. The promise of riches unleashes an incredible drive to create, explore, invent, and build. The result of this activity can improve society immeasurably for everyone. We have experienced this over and over again, from the invention of machines, to the discovery of miracle drugs, to the rise of the internet and beyond.

Capitalism has undeniably improved our quality of life in numerous ways. The free market has made available all sorts of goods and services that we enjoy in our daily lives. We no longer struggle for food, but instead we stop at the grocery store. We no longer suffer from exposure, but instead we throw on a pair of jeans and a sweater. We no longer worry about shelter, but instead we go home to an amazingly safe and comfortable structure. We open the faucet for fresh water. We flick the switch for light, and turn the dial for heat. We click the remote control for a cornucopia of wonderment on our television screens from global news, to sports, to history, to entertainment. We grab our cell phones to share thoughts, photos and videos with networks of our friends and family.

Impressive.

Of course, capitalism alone does not deserve all the credit for all of these wonderful advancements. But capitalism has indeed made many beneficial contributions to society. And we must not lose sight of its tremendous potential for improving our lives.

Having said that, however, we also must acknowledge that capitalism is not perfect. Far from it. In fact, capitalism has serious flaws. It is in part responsible for conquest, war, colonialism, slavery, environmental destruction, pollution, oppression of the masses in appalling labor conditions, excessive consumerism, and the dehumanization of work.

Horrendous.

We must conclude that capitalism is neither all good nor all bad, but that capitalism is simultaneously both good and bad.

3.3   Taming the Beast: Regulation

Western civilization has recognized the dichotomy that capitalism is both a blessing and a curse. Nations that adopted capitalism have typically endeavored to encourage its positive aspects while simultaneously attempting to restrain its wicked aspects.

The positive aspects are pursued simply by turning capitalism loose in society and letting it run wild, create its free markets, and work its magic. At the same time, its negative aspects are restrained by enacting rules and regulations to keep it in check.

Regulations on free markets are necessary. We know this now. We learned it the hard way. In fact, we continue to learn it the hard way over and over again with every recession, scam, scandal, and bust. When the free market is left to its own devices, it inevitably develops atrocious practices that cause substantial damage to society.

The pattern by now is familiar because it repeats over and over again. The free market is turned loose to generate wealth in society. But the free market causes a disaster. Regulations are imposed to patch-up the damage and prevent this particular problem from happening again in the future. We assure ourselves that everything has been fixed. So we set the free market loose again. Very soon another disaster occurs. New regulations are devised and applied. We assure ourselves that everything has now been fixed. We set the free market loose again. Very soon another disaster occurs....

The cycle repeats over and over again.

A basic example from real life of how the free market leads to disaster is the case of monopolies. In a given market, some companies competing against each other will merge to create a larger company that dominates the entire market. This makes sense from a free-market perspective. A larger company can earn more money. So of course this consolidation will occur. This is exactly the type of development that happens in an unregulated free market. But, of course, it leads to all sorts of problems.

The new large company will improperly use its outsized market power against the other small companies, such as by selling products below cost at a loss until all the smaller companies have been driven out of business. Once it eliminates its competitors, the large company becomes a monopoly that rules the entire market all by itself. It erects barriers to entry to block any new competitors from entering the market. It can then dictate prices, which of course means increasing them without limit. Consumers who need the particular products have no choice but to pay the exorbitant prices. This is wonderful for the big company. It earns profits hand over fist. But, of course, the result is disastrous for consumers and society overall.

How do we know that free markets will behave this way and form monopolies? Because we experienced it. The nation unfortunately lived through the problem of monopolies during the rise of the behemoth business trusts in the Gilded Age of the late 1800s and early 1900s.

After decades of this corporate tyranny, the common people finally had enough. Congress eventually enacted the Sherman Antitrust Act in 1890 to break-up the giant trusts and prevent such monopolies from forming in the future. President Theodore "Teddy" Roosevelt (1901-1909) famously took to the warpath on a trust-busting crusade to break apart a number of these big businesses. His successor, President William Taft (1909-1913), continued in his stead.

In the early decades of the 1900s, the Supreme Court broke apart The Standard Oil Company owned by Rockefeller, The American Tobacco Company owned by the Duke family, and the DuPont chemical company, among others. Between the two administrations of Roosevelt and Taft, the federal government brought over one hundred anticompetitive cases against companies in all sorts of industries.

And sometimes, large corporations prevailed over the federal government. The administration of President Taft attempted but failed to break-up the enormous U.S. Steel

Corporation that had been founded by Andrew Carnegie and subsequently bought by J.P. Morgan.

Monopolies serve as a prime example of the recurring pattern. Capitalism is turned loose as a wonderful engine for growth. It creates enormous wealth but also enormous problems. The unfairness persists in society for an extended period of time until it reaches a boiling point. Finally, regulations are enacted to correct the unfairness.

The antitrust laws still exist to this day and are regarded as a fundamental necessity in the regulation of free markets. Without these laws, free-market capitalism would quickly devolve into domination and oppression.

The problem of monopolies is just one instance in a vast ocean of examples. For a grand tour of past disasters caused by the free market just turn to the volume of current regulations as a tour guide. Each regulation was enacted as a corrective response to an actual disaster caused by the free market.

Rules against bid-rigging were enacted because the free market allowed bidders to rig their bids. Rules against insider trading were enacted because the free market allowed company executives to profit from internal company information not yet known to outsiders. Rules against market manipulation were enacted because the free market allowed wealthy players to lock-in profits by trading enormous positions large enough to change the price of a stock. The entire system of financial disclosure requiring companies to file regular reports that must be truthful was enacted because the free market allowed companies to make false or misleading claims about their operations.

The examples are endless. Every regulation exists in response to problems that actually occurred. Just think of all the seemingly infinite regulations regarding virtually every area of corporate endeavor, such as product safety, food safety, chemical safety, pharmaceutical safety, false advertising, usury, truth in lending, home foreclosure laws, food labeling, price fixing, child labor laws, worker protection laws, tenant protection laws, licensing for doctors, insurance fraud, pyramid schemes, bribery, clean water rules, clean air rules, and on and on.

Just think of the extraordinarily massive amounts of fraud, swindles, and damage caused by corporations in order to necessitate this enormous body of regulations. The quantity of wrongdoing exceeds the capacity of the mind to fathom.

And this all makes sense. The free market understands one thing and one thing only: profit.

If an activity makes money, the market pursues it. The market is blind to the fact that human beings even exist. The market has no knowledge of its effects upon people. The market knows nothing of morality, fairness, or suffering.

Dumping toxic chemicals into the river is cheaper, so that is the best course of action. Swindling elderly people out of their life savings is profitable, so go for it. Including a safety measure on a child's toy adds a few extra cents to the production cost, so scrap it.

Left alone, the free market inflicts devastating harm upon human beings. So human beings must erect all sorts of regulations around the free market in an attempt to control it.

The regulatory environment reveals the basic structure of capitalist systems today in the United States as well as around the world. The underlying principle is that free-market capitalism is turned loose in society with the high hopes that it will create wealth. Of course, all sorts of problems ensue and in response individual regulations are enacted to attempt to correct the problems.

So capitalist systems are composed of a free market constituting the essential core of the system, and this core is then surrounded by a massive body of regulations that attempt to keep the system from spinning out of control and wreaking devastation upon society.

It is sort of like trying to tame a powerful wild beast. Left to its own devices, the wild beast would run rampant in an unpredictable manner destroying property and killing people with reckless abandon. The obvious solution would be to banish the beast from the village entirely. Problem solved. The old adage comes to mind that you must kill the beast or the beast will kill you.

But the village people do not kill or banish the beast. They yearn to harness the power of the beast to serve their own interests, such as by, say, plowing their fields. So they keep the beast in the village. They convince themselves that they can control the beast.

They try keeping the beast contained in a pen, inside a barn, or locked in a stable. They try petting it softly, spanking it only delicately, and feeding it as a reward. They experiment with various restraining devices, like a harness around its neck, a bridle bit in its mouth, and reins along its sides.

But the beast invariably finds new ways to break free and cause destruction. In the aftermath of each disaster, the people develop another newfangled fastener to contain the latest breach. Some of these measures work, some do not.

The people intentionally keep this powerful beast close in their midst knowing full well that all their straps and accoutrements may not be able restrain it. The beast remains wild at heart and poses the constant threat of breaking out and inflicting yet another disaster upon the people.

It is a dangerous game. But the people so desperately desire to harness the power of the beast to serve their interests that they are willing to risk the consequences of suffering the wrath of the beast.

Free-market capitalism is the beast, and rules and regulations are the straps and leashes dangling tenuously about it attempting to keep it under control. But these measures often fail.

Nonetheless, many nations around the world, including our own, employ a system of capitalism. Their structures are essentially the same with a free market as the core wrapped by elaborate regulations to contain it. The main difference among the various systems is the nature and extent of the regulations. Some countries impose greater restrictions on the free market and some less.

In one way or another, however, the free market will inevitably elude its restraints and make new mischief.

Today is no exception. In our contemporary time, the free market has once again broken loose and is wreaking havoc upon our society.

The affliction this time around has taken the form of drastic economic inequality.

3.4   Scrap Capitalism Entirely?

Some believe that the problems with capitalism are so pervasive and so deeply embedded that the only way to solve all of the problems would be to eliminate the entire system of capitalism altogether and replace it with something completely new.

This is indeed a legitimate perspective and worthy of consideration. Of course, a replacement system superior to capitalism must first be devised. A consensus, however, has yet to emerge in support of any such replacement. Also, replacing the entire system of capitalism would be an enormous undertaking. The task is so daunting that it almost certainly could not be attempted anytime soon. And even if such an endeavor were attempted, the process would be so long in duration that it would fail to deliver tangible results in the foreseeable future. In the meantime, economic inequality would continue to rage uncontrollably.

While replacing capitalism entirely may well be a worthwhile topic for analysis over the long-term, it is not an ideal solution for the short-term. This writing, therefore, leaves aside any exploration of eliminating capitalism altogether, and instead pursues a course of modifying the existing system of capitalism with the aspiration of achieving a realistic and practical proposal capable of delivering rapid results.

3.5   Easy Diagnosis:
Capital Is Dominating Labor

The problem of economic inequality is simple to assess.

The two central groups in our capitalist economy are "capital" and "labor." Capital represents the owners and investors of the corporations. This also includes the senior executives of the corporations since they are often paid in company stock and thus become significant shareholders (so, also owners). This group of capital constitutes the wealthy 1%.

Labor represents the workers. It also includes most of the managers in the corporations. The workers and the managers perform and manage the actual daily work. They are paid in wages or salaries. While some of these people may also own stock in the corporation, especially the more senior managers, they do not own substantial amounts of stock. Their livelihoods are earned primarily through wages and salary. This group of labor includes the massive middle class. It also includes poor people as well as the unemployed. This labor group constitutes the 99%.

The dynamic between these two groups is that capital and labor are mostly opposed to one another. To be sure, they are not completely opposed. They do share certain interests, particularly in a basic sense. But their relationship is dominated by an inherent and inevitable conflict.

Consider for example a manufacturing plant. In a basic respect, the interests of the owners (capital) and the workers (labor) are aligned. After all, they both desire the plant to exist in the first place, and they both desire the plant to earn enough profit to keep the enterprise operating. Otherwise, the plant would go out of business, in which case the owners would have nothing to own and the workers would have no place to work. So at a basic level, certain interests of the owners and workers are aligned.

But if the plant exists and is profitable, an unavoidable complication arises. The interests of the owners and the workers significantly diverge. The heart of the divergence is how the two groups should share the profits between them. It's all about how to divide-up the kitty.

The owners of the plant desire to maximize their own share of the profits. The owners benefit by minimizing the share that goes to the workers. So the owners desire the workers to work as long and as hard as humanly possible for the lowest possible wages.

The workers, however, desire the exact opposite outcome. They desire to maximize their own share of the profits. The workers benefit by minimizing the share that goes to the owners. So the workers desire to work the least amount at a leisurely pace for the highest possible wages.

And thus lies the inherent conflict between capital and labor.

For the last few decades since approximately the 1980s, capital has been winning the game. Big time.

Slowly but surely, capital has been implementing a barrage of measures to shift more and more of the profits away from labor down below and up into the hands of the wealthy above.

Capital imposed numerous hardships upon labor. These took many forms such as reducing wages, increasing the employee copay in the health insurance plan, eliminating the health insurance plan altogether, cancelling the 401k contribution from the company, eliminating pension plans, destroying labor unions, introducing automation to replace workers, shipping jobs overseas under globalization, downsizing, rightsizing, outsourcing, and flat-out laying-off workers.

These measures reduced the costs of the corporations at the expense of labor, thereby increasing the profits to capital. The increased profits led to increased share prices, further enriching capital.

This effectively constituted an enormous transfer of wealth away from the 99% down below and up to the wealthiest 1% above. The rich grew richer, the middle class declined, and the poor grew poorer.

The overall result has been to leave society plagued with drastic economic inequality.

This is the situation in which we find ourselves today. Capital is dominating labor.

Identifying the problem, however, is the easy part. The difficult part is divining the solution.

Chapter

4

A Problem With No Solution?

We desperately need a solution to our problem of economic inequality. But everywhere we look, no solution can be found.

4.1   Too Big to Fix

Part of the challenge is the sheer enormity of the problem. Economic inequality is everywhere. It is happening all around us. It is attacking us from every direction. It plagues every state, every city, and every town. It is happening in big companies and small companies, in every industry, and in every job function.

Witness the power of the free market.

The marketplace is massive. Just think of all the different kinds of products and services available in the marketplace and all the countless companies that produce them. Food, clothes, automobiles, housing, construction, electronics, healthcare. It is mind-boggling. The economy is enormous.

We typically think of this as positive. All of these goods and services meet the needs of the population and this makes for a productive and healthy society. This theory of the benevolent free market was introduced by the Scottish economist and philosopher Adam Smith back in 1776 in his seminal book, "The Wealth of Nations." This was essentially the first modern work of economics and to this day it serves as the basis of free-market economics.

According to Smith, even though every enterprise throughout the entire marketplace, such as the "butcher, brewer, and baker," act selfishly in their own economic interest to maximize their own profit, society also benefits as well because society receives meat, beer, and bread. It all works out wonderfully all by itself. It's like magic.

As Smith famously described, an "invisible hand" seems to be working behind the scenes to be sure that all the selfish individual profit-making activities by every company in the marketplace also happen to benefit society as well. Thus there is no need for intervention into the workings of the free market. Zero maintenance. The thing flies all by itself. It automatically works wonderfully for everyone.

This all sounds terrific. But what happens if there is a glitch? What happens if companies discover that they can earn greater profits for themselves from activities that do not benefit society but instead that actually harm society? What happens if the "invisible hand" goes rogue and becomes a pickpocket?

What happens if the butcher, brewer, and baker discover that by, say, dumping their toxic waste into the nearby river they could boost their profits even though this dumping would poison the entire community?

We know what happens. It's obvious. Companies will act in their own self-interest. They will do whatever earns them the highest profit regardless of the consequences to society overall. The butcher, brewer, and baker will all dump away with reckless abandon.

If the entire market turns against society, this creates a gigantic problem of enormous proportion. The market is so massive with so many companies that its power is vast. Solving such a problem seems impossible. There are just too many companies to even begin to control.

Welcome to the problem of modern-day economic inequality.

Market forces have incentivized all sorts of companies throughout the entire system to turn against society. Companies can increase their individual profits by suppressing the wages and benefits of their workers to the utter ruination of the middle class. This is now occurring on a massive scale throughout the entire economy. The number of companies engaged in some form of this activity is so widespread that an enormous crisis has developed for society as a whole.

The problem is massive.

How in the world are we supposed to solve something like this? It seems too overwhelming in scale. Far too many companies are involved to address each one of them. It's difficult to see where to even begin.

But one aspect seems apparent. The overall problem will never be conquered by small, individual programs. It would be futile to provide a tax break for this particular subgroup or a bit of financial assistance for that particular subgroup.

A piecemeal approach of applying one little patch here and another little patch there would never be sufficient.

Instead, the solution must rise to the enormity of the problem. The problem lies with the entire market itself. Companies are currently incentivized throughout the system to exploit their workers. So the solution must also be directed at the entire market. Companies somehow must be deterred from squeezing their workers and instead be rewarded for caring for their workers on a market-wide basis.

Devising such a large-scale solution is daunting.

4.2   The Free Market Offers No Answer

According to traditional free-market theory, the free market is supposed to solve economic problems in society all on its own.

To be fair to free-market devotees, the market does in fact solve many problems on its own. If a shortage of a product occurs, the market responds. Demand increases, which in turn causes prices to rise, which in turn causes producers to increase supplies, and thereby the shortage is eliminated. The free market can also be effective at establishing prices because it provides a mechanism where many sellers can ask for their desired prices and many buyers can bid with their desired counter-prices. Through this robust bidding process, the actual price emerges somewhere in between. So the free market indeed performs valuable functions.

But in the case of economic inequality, the free market is not solving this problem on its own. Not hardly. In fact, the free market is what got us into this mess in the first place. Market forces are exactly what led to the shifting of great wealth away from the lower 99% and up into the hands of the 1%.

When it comes to economic inequality, the free market has failed us. The problem is not being solved. Once we accept this fact, then we realize something significant. The problem is not going to turn around on its own. It will not fix itself. If we stand by and do nothing, the situation will never improve and will likely only become worse.

We now realize that intervention is required. Changes must be made. A plan must be devised.

4.3   Too Tough a Problem for the Rich

In order to solve the nasty problem of economic inequality, maybe we should turn to the rich people at the top of the economy and ask for their assistance.

Rich people certainly possess the requisite expertise. They are making all the money. They control the corporations. And their corporations generate all the revenue and make the crucial decisions of how this revenue is apportioned and shared among the stakeholders of the workers, the managers, the executives, and the shareholders.

Terrific! The rich seem to be exactly the type of experts we need.

So what do the rich say when asked how to solve the problem of economic inequality?

"Oh, gee," they say, "that's a tough one. It certainly is quite a problem. But gosh, it just seems so complicated. So difficult. So many different factors. Oh goodness gracious. It's just so hard to understand. We have no idea what in the world could be causing economic inequality. Boy, oh, boy, we sure wish we could help out more. It's just that the problem is way too hard for us to solve. So sorry. But we wish you the best of luck!"

Hm. That's curious. Even the most wealthy and powerful people in society have no idea how to solve the problem. The very people who make the decisions about how to distribute the money have no solutions for how to distribute it more fairly.

Really? Could this be possible? The very people who allocate the money have no idea why a precious few receive far too much (ahem, themselves), and the great masses of people receive far too little? Really? No idea?

Hmmm....

4.4   Politicians Come Up Empty

Since neither the free market nor the wealthy business people are solving economic inequality, we are left to turn to the political process for relief.

The job of politicians is to solve problems in society. But in this case, the politicians have offered no adequate solutions to economic inequality.

This is astonishing. After all, economic inequality is an enormous problem that plagues the overwhelming majority of people in our society. This should present a golden opportunity for ambitious politicians eager to make a name for themselves. Offering a solution to economic inequality would propel candidates directly into office. It is a ticket to the top. The wizard who solves this problem would be heralded as a true champion of the people, and even celebrated as having delivered one of the greatest advancements in the history of our society.

Yet politicians offer zippo.

To be fair, some politicians have attempted to seize upon this issue. Some have even been genuine and passionate in articulating the problem of how income inequality is plaguing our society.

They capture our attention. We think to ourselves, hey, this candidate seems to understand our plight. They rail against the unfairness in society. Yes! They decry the obscene accumulation of wealth. Exactly! They lambast the absurd concentration of power. Yes yes yes!

They pledge to correct this awful scourge on society. Fantastic!

They announce their proposed solution with great thunder: An increase in the earned income tax credit!

Huh?

Crickets.

What the heck good will that do? Sure, it would no doubt benefit some people here and there to some extent, but it is the equivalent of adding a single grain of sand to a beach that is being inundated by a giant tsunami. It is wholly inadequate to the enormity of the problem.

A number of other proposals have been offered as well that similarly fall short in magnitude. Some proposals would increase the minimum wage, or offer free college tuition at community colleges. Others would provide assistance for childcare, or retrain workers for high-technology jobs.

These types of programs are all fine and good. But they are not big enough. Not bold enough. They barely scratch the surface. They clearly do not come anywhere close to solving the enormous problem of economic inequality that pervades our society. People know right away that reforms like these are not sufficient to make a meaningful difference in their lives.

So the politicians have nothing to offer.

This is amazing. But it's true. There are no politicians who are offering any sort of a realistic solution to economic inequality.

Why? How can this be possible? Why? Why? Why?

Hmmm....

4.5   Circle of Exclusion

Hold on a second here. Something does not seem right. Are we being deceived? Duped? Bamboozled?

The wealthy must certainly know how resources could be distributed more fairly in society. They know how the money is made, and they control how it is allocated. Of course they know how to fix this problem!

So why are the wealthy not stepping-up and offering solutions to economic inequality?

Simple. The wealthy have no incentive to fix the problem. In fact, the exact opposite is the case. The wealthy have every incentive to perpetuate the problem.

Who benefits the most from this unfair system? Of course, it is the wealthy. The current system is what makes them wealthy. Even though the system is broken and drastically unfair to the vast majority of people, this dysfunction is precisely what rewards the wealthy. So the wealthy do not wish to fix the problem. They have no reason to change the system. Instead, they have every reason to keep it exactly the way it is.

Okay. So that explains the wealthy. We certainly cannot expect them to be helpful.

But what about the politicians? Why are they not stepping-up to solve economic inequality?

It is possible that the politicians simply do not have the expertise to know how to fix the problem. After all, most of them have no experience in big business or high finance. Without the necessary knowledge, they are unable to devise effective solutions.

Is this believable? For many individual congresspersons, this explanation is likely legitimate. They simply do not possess the wherewithal to tackle such an enormous societal problem as economic inequality.

But Congress as a whole is a different matter. Congress is a large body with considerable powers and extraordinary resources. Therefore, it seems unlikely that the entire body of Congress would be unable to produce effective solutions. There must be more to the story.

As it just so happens, politicians have a perverse incentive as well.

In the modern age, political campaigns have become ever more expensive. A critical factor for every candidate has become their ability to raise funds. If a politician cannot raise funds, then they cannot be elected. And once in office, if they cannot continue to raise funds, then they cannot remain in office by being reelected.

Where do candidates turn to raise their funds? Naturally, they turn to people who possess funds. And this of course is the wealthy. As a whole, politicians have developed an extraordinary dependency upon the wealthy. This in turn shapes the policies of the politicians. They cannot readily adopt policies that are adverse to their wealthy donors or they will soon find themselves without any donors and swiftly out of office.

So how in the world can politicians seek to end economic inequality when their own wealthy donors favor preserving economic inequality?

The answer, of course, is that they cannot. Our campaign finance system is broken.

No wonder politicians do not offer any realistic solutions for ending economic inequality. Politicians simply cannot advocate for positions that so threaten the entire class of their wealthy donors.

It is a vicious circle. The wealthy will not fix economic inequality because they benefit from it. And the politicians will not fix economic inequality because they cannot oppose the wealthy. There is nowhere left to turn for relief.

The unholy alliance between the wealthy and the politicians has created a powerful force. It is a self-reinforcing loop. A circle of exclusion. This alliance has created an economic system that is extremely unfair for almost everyone in society. And it blocks all the pathways to reforming the system. There is no way in.

It is like a great castle surrounded by high walls that keep out the middle class and the poor. Inside the walls, the wealthy and the politicians enjoy the great comfort of financial security. Outside the walls, the rest of the people are forced to struggle just to get by.

Remarkably, in broad daylight, in what is supposedly the greatest democracy in the world, the vast majority of the people are suffering unfairly and have been shut-out from the system.

4.6 Broken Society

The problem of economic inequality compels us to look in the mirror and confront some very serious questions about our cherished system of government. We see in the reflection that our society is not functioning properly. And we see that our system is unable to solve the problem. We cannot help but consider the uncomfortable reality that our system is not the model of fairness we always thought it to be. We cannot avoid the unthinkable question of whether our system is even a democracy.

A democratic society possesses the ability to solve its own problems. Indeed, this is the whole point. Under a monarchy, the king rules everything by personal fiat, and the people have no say in the matter. But in a democracy, if the leaders are failing to solve a problem in society, the people can vote those leaders out of office and replace them with new leaders who will solve the problem. This is the essence of democracy.

Of course, even the most democratic of societies will still have problems. Smaller problems in particular might not rise to the level of warranting governmental action.

But the economic inequality that plagues our society today is no small matter. It is not just something at the margins. It is not a mere technicality. It is not some sort of a glitch. It is not just an aberration. Economic inequality is an enormous problem. The entire middle class is under assault. The standard of living has eroded. Poor people are suffering grievously.

The economic system itself has been hijacked and is now operating primarily for the benefit of only the wealthy few at the top while the overwhelming majority of people are unsatisfied and left to struggle.

The problem pervades our entire system and thus is one of the greatest issues confronting our overall society.

So how has our system responded?

Surprisingly, it has not responded in a way that we would expect for a democracy. It has not attempted to solve the problem. Instead, it has acted in the opposite manner.

The system has shaped itself into a self-protecting defensive formation that seeks to preserve the unfairness. The alliance between the wealthy and the politicians has been extremely effective. They have circled the wagons. The system has blocked all the pathways to reform. There appears to be no way to change the system. The vast majority of people have been locked-out and left helpless.

This is hardly democratic. Indeed, in a proper democracy, elected representatives of the people would offer proposals on behalf of their constituents to solve economic inequality. Instead, however, our elected representatives have aligned themselves with the interests of the wealthy few at the top to prevent reforms that would benefit the suffering population.

This is more reflective of the conduct of an oligarchy, not a democracy. In an oligarchy, a small group of rich people at the top control the entire society and subject the rest of the population to oppression.

Unfortunately, this is all too recognizable in our society today.

We are left with a system that is plagued with economic inequality on an enormous scale, and no way to solve the problem.

When a society is unable to solve its biggest problems, that society is broken.

The United States of America, in the dawn of the twenty-first century, is broken.

Chapter

5

Ready for Revolution!

What happens when society is not working properly? What happens when the people are treated unfairly? What happens when a wealthy aristocracy plunders society for its own avarice?

5.1 Our Past Reveals Our Future

History teaches us what happens when the population has finally had enough of being oppressed by an unfair government. The common people join together, rise up in revolution, and overthrow their rulers.

A prime example of this is the French Revolution in 1789 when the peasants rose up and overthrew the French monarchy. Ultimately, this revolution led to a democracy in France.

In fact, the French Revolution inspired a wave of revolutions and reforms in nation after nation around the world that resulted in the decline of absolute monarchies and the rise of governments that were more fair to common individuals.

Our very own beloved nation was created by exactly this sort of revolution. In 1776, the American colonists had been oppressed for long enough by the king of England, George III. The colonists declared independence from England and fought the American Revolution to obtain the freedoms that we enjoy today.

It is now time for a second revolution in America. Once again, the people must rise up to free themselves from the chains of economic inequality.

Fortunately, the revolution of today does not require violence. People do not need to take up arms or storm government buildings. This is because people today possess a powerful instrument that was not available to the revolutionaries of the past. Namely, the right to vote.

5.2   Go Big and Bold

How in the world could the powerless people today ever overcome the extremely powerful people at the top?

It is a daunting task. The alliance between the wealthy and the politicians seems to have everything all locked-up by keeping the rest of us all locked-out. It makes us want to just give up and accept our discontent. Economic inequality appears to have no solution. It seems impossible.

But it's not impossible.

We can find a way. We must find a way.

We cannot aim small. We will not be satisfied with mere crumbs. We will not be appeased with modest reforms here and there that might make incremental improvements at the margins. No. We are after much more.

Our approach must be big and bold. Our goal is to solve the problem. The entire problem. Big problems require big solutions.

Our proposal will be radical. It must be radical. It must be powerful enough to break through the sturdy walls erected by the wealthy to exclude the common people.

Our proposal will be extreme. It must be extreme. It must be strong enough to force the rich to share a portion of their wealth with the rest of society to achieve a more equitable balance.

We will be courageous. We must be courageous. We must persevere through the onslaught of attacks by wealthy interests that will seek to crush our reforms.

The rich and powerful at the top will hear our roar from down below: No Solution? Revolution!

Chapter

6

Conscript the Rich

These are the times that try rich people's souls.

If the American revolutionary Thomas Paine were here today, he would call upon the rich to perform their duty. As he expressed, no one may shrink from the service of their country, and those who expect to reap the blessings of freedom must, with valor, undergo the fatigue of supporting it.

Back then, Paine was calling upon American colonists to join the army to fight for independence from England in order to create a free society. Today, Paine would be calling upon the wealthy to share some of their riches in order to preserve this free society.

6.1   Mandatory Volunteers

In one way or another, by hook or by crook, the wealthy will be part of any solution.

The reason is plain. The rich have all the money. So any solution will necessarily involve some form of the Robin Hood principle of interceding in the flow of excess money to the rich and redirecting a portion of it to the rest of society.

So it is unavoidable that the rich will be affected.

At first blush, conscripting the rich might seem like a drastic measure. America is based upon the principle of freedom, so we tend to shy away from forcing people to take action against their will.

But upon reflection, conscripting the rich reveals itself as eminently justified. After all, the rich have been conscripting the common people for ages. This, in fact, is how they became rich.

Certainly, workers have been conscripted into their jobs by economic circumstances. They have been forced to toil away for long hours and meager earnings while owners at the top have become wealthy. But also, just about every fortune can be traced to dollars that in one way or another have come from the common people. Fortunes at the top consist of money that has been funneled upward from ordinary people down below.

Because the conscription of common people into labor enables the great accumulation of wealth in the hands of a small minority of rich people, it is perfectly reasonable to turn the tables and conscript the rich into the effort of assisting the common people who made them rich in the first place.

When the rich wail and moan about unfair "redistribution" of their money downward to the common people, we must not be fooled. This money was generated in the first instance by the labor of the workers and never should have been distributed up to the wealthy in the first place. So the "redistribution" downward is merely correcting the injustice of a prior distribution upward.

6.2   Open Arms

The wealthy must be extended a warm invitation to participate in the process of devising the solution to economic inequality. While the voluntary participation of the wealthy is not absolutely necessary, it is highly preferable. Thus an important objective of any initiative should be to encourage the wealthy to join the process.

The wealthy could be extremely helpful in developing the solution. After all, they possess a high degree of expertise about the workings of business and finance. So their contributions could be of great value.

Additionally, if the wealthy participated in the process, they would become invested in the solution. They would become more likely to actively participate in the design of the solution and in its implementation on an ongoing basis. The wealthy would become a stakeholder in making the solution work, and this would enhance the likelihood of success as well as foster greater cohesiveness in society.

Including the wealthy in the process will face obstacles. Initially, the wealthy will be vehemently opposed to the overall effort to solve economic inequality because any solution would likely threaten to reduce their wealth. So initially, the wealthy will fight ferociously to quash the effort entirely.

But once they are unsuccessful at stopping it, the wealthy would then likely reverse their position and instead participate in the process voluntarily. As the saying goes, if you can't beat 'em, join 'em. And nothing less than their wealth is at stake so they will wish to have a voice in the process. They will desire to influence the outcome. They will conclude that it is far better to have a seat at the table than to leave their fate entirely in the hands of others.

Let us have no illusions. The wealthy will be less than enthusiastic about participating in a process that threatens to reduce their wealth. So they might prove to be disruptive from within by sabotaging proposals and undermining solutions in order to preserve the status quo. Such behavior should be anticipated, identified, and overcome. Despite the potential for disruption, the wealthy should be included nonetheless.

The process should be designed to encourage the wealthy to participate and contribute positively.

Chapter

7

The Power of Incentives

How can the wealthy be forced to participate in solving economic inequality?

We would certainly not seek to compel their participation by physical force. They would not be led off in chains or tossed in the clink if they refused to show up for meetings.

Instead, the rich would be induced to participate through proper incentives.

It's all about incentives.

7.1   Destructive Incentives

The current incentive structure in our society is upside down. There are no financial incentives for anyone to solve the underlying forces that are causing economic inequality. Zero. No one can become rich by solving this problem. Even if the greatest thinker of our age devised an ingenious solution, there would be no way for her to make money from it, and thus no market application for it. So no one attempts to do it.

On the other hand, there are gigantic financial incentives to worsen economic inequality. The entire financial system with all its massive power is uniformly concentrated on exacerbating inequality.

Numerous corporate executives all across the nation are paid millions of dollars to devise ever more shrewd methods of making life worse and worse for their workers and society overall. Their objective, of course, is not presented in such direct terms. Instead, their overt objective is to increase the profits of their corporations, especially the short-term profits, or else they might be fired and replaced.

A quick and easy way for executives to increase profits is to cut expenses. The standard playbook for achieving this is to impose cuts upon the great many workers. This can take numerous different forms, such as reducing wages, eliminating benefits, terminating pension plans, introducing automation to replace workers, outsourcing jobs to contract workers, sending jobs overseas under globalization, and just plain old-fashioned lay-offs.

When these measures reduce expenses, corporate profits increase and the executives are rewarded with millions of dollars. And when corporate profits increase, the share price increases as well and the shareholders are rewarded with millions of dollars of their own.

We see this frequently in the news. When headlines announce that a corporation is laying-off workers, one might think this would be bad news for the company and that the stock price of the company would drop. But instead, the exact opposite occurs. Investors love it. Fewer workers means lower costs and this means greater profits for investors. So the lay-offs actually cause the company stock price to increase.

Talk about an upside down system!

The rich get richer. But it all comes at the expense of the workers. They get poorer. The middle class erodes, economic inequality worsens, and society falls into decline.

Incentives are also misaligned in terms of career paths within corporate America. The best and brightest young minds graduating from our finest universities desire to earn the most money for themselves, so they go to work for corporations that offer the largest earning potential. As their careers advance, they follow the well-trodden path to wealth forged by their bosses, who teach them the ropes. So they too engage in similar cost-cutting and other techniques to increase profitability at the expense of the workers and the communities.

Instead of our best and brightest people dedicating their great passions and abilities to benefitting society by solving its biggest problems, they do the exact opposite. They instead take jobs that pay the most money but that worsen society's problems. The cycle continues from one generation to the next with society suffering more and more.

And what happens when these people finally reach the top and attain their wealth? Do they then change their ways and try to improve society by ending all the harmful practices? Well, no.

Instead, they seek to protect the system that is making them richer and richer. They use their wealth to influence the political process to prevent reform. Not only do they not help to reduce economic inequality, but instead they actively work to perpetuate the unfairness by opposing attempts at meaningful change.

So, society's best and brightest become society's richest and most powerful, and then they use their wealth and power to entrench themselves and perpetuate the dysfunction.

It is a self-reinforcing system. No wonder we have a breakdown. No wonder society is suffering. No wonder economic inequality has drastically increased over the last several decades with no end in sight.

The incentives are backwards. Upside down. Haywire.

7.2   Constructive Incentives

The system needs a tune-up. We must turn things around and implement positive incentives. The wealthy must be induced to stop being part of the problem and start being part of the solution.

The proper incentive structure is easy to envision. The system must be corrected so that the wealthy would stand to gain financially if economic inequality were brought into balance. And by the same token, if economic inequality were not brought into balance, then the wealthy would stand to lose financially.

A powerful tool for creating financial incentives is the tax code. In this situation, the tax code could be utilized to incentivize the wealthy to solve income inequality. If economic inequality is not solved by a specified future date, the wealthy would become subject to a higher tax rate.

This alone would cause the wealthy to perk-up and suddenly take economic inequality seriously. For the first time, this problem would now threaten to harm their income.

In order to constitute a sufficient incentive, the tax must be substantial. It must be high enough that it would materially impact the income of the wealthy. Only then would the wealthy be incentivized to help solve the problem.

When faced with the prospect of such a tax, the wealthy would be willing to sacrifice a portion of their own income and contribute it to the problem, in theory, up to the amount of the tax. They would also participate in crafting the solution. And they would continue their involvement throughout the implementation of the solution as well. After all, they would wish to ensure that any solution would actually be successful in order to avoid the dreaded tax on themselves.

Utilizing the tax code to create incentives would indeed affect the behavior of the wealthy.

Incentives are powerful tools.

With the proper incentives in place, all of a sudden the wealthy would show up bright-eyed and bushy-tailed all ready to get to work to solve economic inequality. We would suddenly see from them a spirit of egalitarianism and passionate concern for common people like never before.

Chapter

8

The Magic Solution: Mend or Spend

The policy solution for ending economic inequality is "Mend or Spend."

The idea is simple. The wealthy would be given a choice. They can choose either to "mend" the problem of economic inequality, or to "spend" by contributing money that would then be applied to solving economic inequality.

If the wealthy chose to "mend," then they would voluntarily participate in a process designed to solve economic inequality. The wealthy would work together with a Committee of Experts to develop a set of policy programs that could be implemented quickly in order to improve economic inequality throughout society.

Or, the wealthy could instead choose to "spend." In this case, the wealthy need not participate at all. But if economic inequality failed to improve before certain predetermined milestones in the future, then the wealthy would be forced to "spend" their own money through the imposition of a substantially higher top marginal income tax rate (applied only to the wealthy, not to the middle class). This revenue would then be used to fund social programs designed to assist the middle class and below.

If the wealthy chose to "Mend" and were able to successfully improve economic inequality, then the wealthy would avoid triggering the "Spend" of the substantial tax on their incomes. Otherwise, the "Spend" component would take effect and the wealthy would be taxed to benefit the common people. One way or the other, economic inequality would be improved and greater fairness in society would be achieved.

Mend or Spend. Plain and simple. Yet it is extraordinarily powerful for solving economic inequality.

Chapter

9

The Mechanics:
How Does It Work?

The rubric of Mend or Spend is not a Rubik's Cube or a Rube Goldberg contraption. The plan is simple, efficient, and effective.

9.1   Who Are the Wealthy?

Who, exactly, are "the wealthy?"

This is a pertinent question because this is the group that would be significantly affected by the Mend or Spend program. The simplest description of this group is those who would be subjected to the higher income tax rate under the "Spend" portion of the policy.

This group would be limited to a small percentage of the population, say the top one or two percent, that receives a disproportionate share of the nation's income. The parameters defining who would be included in the taxed group would be set forth in the initial legislation. The tax would apply to all income above a threshold amount, say, perhaps $1 million per year, or maybe $5 million, or perhaps $10 million per year.

Sorry wealthy people, but there will be no loopholes to exploit. All types of income will be subject to the higher tax rate, including long-term capital gains, corporate dividends, income from "pass-through" entities, and "carried interest" from private equity funds.

Taxation, of course, would remain "progressive" so that the new tax would be applied only to the portion of a person's income above the threshold. The portion of the person's income below the threshold would still be taxed at the lower ordinary rates.

How are the wealthy expected to make the decision of whether to "Mend" or "Spend?" And if they chose to "Mend," how would they participate?

Simple. It's all up to them.

Anyone and everyone is free to decide for themselves whether to participate. Some might choose to participate, others not. Knock yourself out.

In practice, the wealthy would likely form themselves into various groups, similar to industry trade associations, in order to coordinate their participation.

In fact, participation would not be limited to only the wealthy. Anyone in society would be welcome to participate by submitting their ideas for how to solve economic inequality. The Committee of Experts would conduct an organized process to include public input similar in nature to the public comment periods when government agencies propose major new regulations. Come one, come all. Good ideas emerge from all quarters.

Regardless of participation, however, one aspect remains constant. The group of wealthy persons subject to the new tax would not change. If the tax were triggered, every person in the wealthy group would be subjected to the tax regardless of whether they had chosen to "Mend" and regardless of whether they had participated in the process.

9.2   What Does It Mean to "Mend?"

For the rich people who chose to "Mend," how would they participate?

Simple. Any way they like.

Participation is purely voluntary. There is no formal process for electing or declining to participate. There are no forms to complete, no filings to make, and no registrations to submit. Nothing of the sort. People are simply free to participate by engaging in any activities they desire.

Some people might submit a letter to the Committee of Experts outlining their ideas for how to solve economic inequality. Other people might attend public hearings of the Committee and voice their thoughts during question-and-answer sessions. The more active participants would likely organize themselves into groups, work with their members to develop a formal written proposal, and submit their proposal to the Committee.

What kinds of suggestions would be permitted?

Anything and everything.

People are free to offer any suggestions they desire. Proposals might include raising the minimum wage, subsidizing daycare, expanding food stamps, "means testing" social security, creating a new national pension program, offering tax cuts for the middle class, providing guaranteed employment, enacting universal healthcare, providing free education, implementing rent regulation, eliminating laws that impede labor unions, and anything else in between or beyond.

Perhaps the wealthy could address the problem of workers who have been left behind by the changing economy, such as those who lost their jobs as a result of new technologies or manufacturing plants being shut down and relocated overseas under globalization. This is a particular problem in rural areas where a plant closure can devastate an entire community. Perhaps the wealthy might propose a new government program to put these people back to work, such as the agencies created by President Franklin Delano Roosevelt (1933-1945) in the 1930s in the aftermath of the Great Depression such as the Works Progress Administration (WPA) and the Civilian Conservation Corps (CCC) that created millions of jobs.

Any and all proposals would be welcome.

Rich people may not like some of these proposals, such as enabling labor unions, and thus they would be loath to recommend them. But rich people will need to decide for themselves where to draw the lines. Is it better to allow labor unions, or be hit with the large new tax? Is it better to increase food stamps, or pay the tax?

As part of their plan, rich people would need to specify how their recommendations would be funded, and this would likely require them to raise taxes on themselves.

At first blush this might seem impossible. Why in the world would rich people raise their own taxes? But the answer is actually quite rational.

If rich people did not raise enough money to adequately solve economic inequality, then their "Mend" proposals would fail and the new tax rate under the "Spend" component would be imposed upon them involuntarily. This rate would far exceed the rate that they would voluntarily impose upon themselves. So it would be perfectly rational for the rich to voluntarily raise their own taxes to, say, 50%, 60%, or 70% in order to avoid the imposition of an involuntary tax that would be even higher.

How would we determine whether the "Mend" proposals have succeeded or failed?

Measuring success is a crucial component to the program because this will determine whether and when to trigger the substantial new tax.

The actual requirements will be determined by the Committee of Experts, but certain aspects seem so fundamental that they almost certainly will apply. The Committee could be expected to set milestone markers at regular intervals of time into the future. The Committee would also create a set of metrics for measuring the extent of economic inequality in the economy, such as ratios and other indicators. And the Committee would establish financial targets applicable to each milestone.

Once the plan has been deployed in society, at every milestone on an ongoing basis, the economy would be measured and evaluated against the predetermined financial targets to assess whether the actions taken were succeeding or failing.

If the financial targets were not met, this would indicate that the plan was not succeeding, and thus this would trigger the imposition of the higher tax rate on the wealthy.

9.3   What Does It Mean to "Spend?"

If the "Spend" component were triggered, then a new income tax rate would automatically become effective.

The change would be an increase to the top marginal income tax rate. So the tax would apply only to the wealthy, and not to the middle class or below.

The new tax rate would be high. Very high. Let's call it, say, 90 percent.

Yes, that's right. A 90 percent tax rate. We're not fooling around here. The tax must be high enough for the wealthy to take it seriously. They must be given a very strong incentive to help solve income inequality. Without this significant motivator, the wealthy would never make a sincere effort. This measure provides a touch of encouragement for them to do the right thing. Nothing sharpens the mind of the wealthy like the prospect of a stiff tax.

The tax would be only temporary until certain financial targets indicate the attainment of an acceptable low level of economic inequality in society.

The objective of Mend or Spend is not to achieve exact equality among every individual. No. The idea is not to create some sort of bizarre society where no one can own more wealth than anyone else. That would be ridiculous.

Rather, the objective is merely to seek a more equitable balance among the rich, the middle class, and the poor.

There will certainly be large differences in earnings and wealth throughout society, but just not excessive inequality. Individuals could still become rich in society, but only after the population as a whole is financially secure.

It is also worth noting that Mend or Spend does not call for a tax on wealth. It does not seek to strip away assets from the wealthy that they already own. Instead, the remedy is a tax on income to more equitably distribute future flows of funds.

Some may contend that taxing only income instead of also taxing accumulated wealth will not generate sufficient funds to solve economic inequality in its entirety. Even if true, this is of no moment. Any amount of funds dedicated to the problem of economic inequality would be an improvement. And the amount from just the income tax would indeed be enormous. So this amount should be marshalled and applied, and the effects should be measured and assessed.

Further, Mend or Spend creates the proper incentive structure for the private sector to actually contend with the problem. This factor is tremendously significant in itself.

If the "Spend" component were ever triggered and the rich all across America were suddenly subject to a 90 percent tax on their incomes, they would not just sit by idly and resign themselves to paying the tax indefinitely into the future. Not a chance.

Instead, the rich would be properly incentivized to solve the problem. The rich would know that if economic inequality were reduced then the tax would be lifted. So the rich would jump from their seats and spring into action. They would join forces with each other and work around the clock as hard as humanly possible to resolve the situation.

Incidentally, all of this hard work would be for the benefit of society overall. The rich would be working for the middle class and the poor. When have we ever seen that?

All of this hard work would greatly increase the likelihood of actually solving economic inequality for society. And this is exactly the point. Even if the revenue from the new tax were insufficient alone to solve the problem, the new tax would still create the proper incentive for solving the problem. The great power of the free market – creating wealth – would be unleashed on the problem of economic inequality. As people begin to innovate and apply new solutions, greater and greater improvements in the economy would materialize.

The proper incentive would be in place to move the economy in the desired direction. Currently, no incentives exist for solving economic inequality. So introducing the correct incentive structure is a critical factor. This alone is enough of a reason to justify implementing the policy.

Mend or Spend declares that wealth shall no longer be achieved by exploiting the common people, but instead, wealth can be achieved only after the common people are financially secure and society as a whole is sound. Under this approach, the best and the brightest people will first be required to ensure that our society is healthy before seeking to attain riches for themselves.

Some might contend that while the 90 percent tax may be appropriate to apply to the established wealthy, it harbors the potential to create unfairness for those who are newly becoming wealthy for the first time by a single event.

Take, for example, an inventor of modest means who toiled for decades on a miraculous invention that benefits all of humanity. When the invention is finally perfected and brought to market, it hardly seems fair to take away 90 percent of the rewards. Or, consider the lottery. The purpose of the lottery would be defeated if 90 percent of the winnings were forfeited. Alternatively, however, if an existing billionaire won the lottery or invented a product, then the 90 percent tax should apply.

These considerations and others are legitimate and would be addressed by the Committee of Experts, such as by applying a net worth metric to allow a greater portion of newfound single-event wealth to be retained.

In the event the "Spend" component were triggered, how would the resulting tax revenue be spent?

This question would be part of the responsibilities of the Committee of Experts. The Committee would develop a plan for applying the funds. A set of new and existing programs would be designated in advance to receive funding. These programs would be designed or selected on the basis of their ability to assist the middle class and the poor in order to reduce the imbalance of economic inequality. The Committee would maintain ongoing oversight to ensure the effectiveness of these programs and to fund new programs as appropriate.

9.4   How Is "Spend" Triggered?

First of all, let us keep in mind that the "Spend" component may never be triggered at all.

The "Mend" component would first go into effect by itself and would be given an opportunity to succeed. During this phase, voluntary measures would be implemented in the economy, and the wealthy would be warmly welcomed to participate in this process. It would indeed be marvelous if the entire problem of economic inequality were solved voluntarily under the "Mend" component. Then the "Spend" component would never need to take effect.

But in the event the voluntary measures under the "Mend" component failed to solve the problem of economic inequality, then the "Spend" component would be standing by, ready, willing, and able to rush to the rescue.

Whether and when the "Spend" component is triggered would be determined by objective measurements pursuant to a predefined overall framework plan issued by the Committee of Experts.

The framework plan would set forth milestones at various points of time into the future. At each milestone, measurements of the economy would be taken to measure the extent of economic inequality. The framework plan would also set forth financial targets applicable to each milestone.

At each milestone in time, if the applicable financial targets were satisfied, this would indicate that economic inequality had been reduced to an acceptable low level and thus was "in balance," in which case the "Spend" component would not be triggered.

Alternatively, if the applicable financial targets were not satisfied at the given milestone, this would indicate that economic inequality was at an unacceptable high level and thus was "out of balance," in which case the "Spend" component would be triggered.

In the event the "Spend" component had been triggered and was in effect, but thereafter at a subsequent milestone economic inequality was brought into balance, then the "Spend" component would be lifted. If, at a future milestone, the measurements again fell out of balance, then the "Spend" component would again be triggered. The measurement process would continue into the future on an ongoing basis and the "Spend" component would be triggered or lifted as required depending upon whether the economy was in balance or out of balance.

Once the framework plan is established, then the program would be administered according to the plan.

But what if the framework plan is never established?

This, unfortunately, is a realistic possibility. One can easily foresee such great squabbling and acrimony that a consensus might never be achieved on how best to solve economic inequality. In such a case, the voluntary proposals of the framework plan might never be formed.

Or perhaps all the bickering could hopelessly delay the framework plan from being issued. Delay, of course, would be a tempting sabotage tactic to the wealthy interests opposed to Mend or Spend. If they could simply prevent the framework plan from being finalized, then perhaps they could indefinitely delay Mend or Spend and thereby effectively abolish it.

Mend or Spend, however, must not be susceptible to being delayed, derailed, or sabotaged.

To prevent delays, an outside trigger date must be established upfront. This trigger date must be established at the very beginning when the Mend or Spend legislation is first enacted, say, at two years after enactment.

At this trigger date, the "Spend" component would automatically take effect. The trigger date would serve as a bright line for all to see. The only possible circumstance that could prevent the "Spend" component from taking effect on the trigger date is if economic inequality were determined to be "in balance" under a framework plan.

Establishing this trigger date upfront would prevent any and all delays. Nothing in the world could stop the "Spend" component from taking effect on the trigger date (except, of course, if economic inequality were "in balance"). Bickering could not stop it. Sabotage could not stop it. Delays could not stop it. Even the failure to issue a framework plan could not stop it.

On the trigger date, come hell or high water, the "Spend" component would be triggered automatically and the stiff new tax rate on the wealthy would take effect.

Establishing this hard-and-fast deadline upfront is critical because it effectively starts a ticking clock for solving the problem. The looming deadline is the key to inspiring the private sector to immediately spring into action and dedicate themselves to creating a solution.

Even if the framework plan were hopelessly mired in disputes and thus had not been created by the trigger date, no problem. The "Spend" component would still be triggered and the new tax rate would still go into effect regardless. The parties could continue to negotiate to form the framework plan after the tax had already taken effect. But it is essential that no delays or extensions apply to the triggering of the "Spend" component. It is preferable to implement the tax sooner rather than later.

The urgency of economic inequality requires the prompt commencement of the remedy.

9.5   Committee of Experts

A central component of the Mend or Spend program is the Committee of Experts.

The Committee is the overall governing body of the entire Mend or Spend program. The Committee is key in many respects as it is responsible for a number of crucial aspects of the program.

The Committee will determine who is included in the group of wealthy citizens that would be subject to the tax increase under the "Spend" component of the program. The Committee would accomplish this by setting the threshold income amount above which the new marginal tax rate would apply.

The Committee is responsible for creating an overall framework plan for solving economic inequality. This plan would be in the form of a written report. The plan would be comprised of a set of numerous individual policy programs and instructions for their implementation.

The Committee would establish and run a process for generating the framework plan. The process would be open and the Committee would consult with members of the public, including the group of wealthy citizens who would be subject to the new tax rate under the "Spend" component of the program. The Committee would establish procedures under which members of the public could submit written recommendations, much like the public comment periods when government agencies propose major new regulations. The Committee would also establish a series of public hearings and question-and-answer sessions.

As part of the Committee's plan, the Committee would establish milestone markers at regular time intervals into the future. The Committee would also devise a set of metrics to measure the extent of economic inequality in the economy. And the Committee would set financial targets applicable to each milestone that would define the acceptable level of inequality.

In the future, at each milestone, the Committee would measure the amount of inequality in the economy. If the measurements failed to satisfy the financial targets applicable to that milestone, then the new higher tax rate under the "Spend" component would be triggered.

In the event the "Spend" component were triggered, the Committee would implement, fund, and oversee a set of new policy programs that would go into effect in accordance with the Committee's plan. These new programs would be funded by the new tax revenue and would be designed to reduce economic inequality by assisting the middle class and below.

Membership of the Committee would be comprised of experts in their fields such as economists, academics, public servants, executives, and policy specialists. The Committee would be free to establish various subcommittees.

The economic perspective of the Committee is absolutely critical. The Committee must not be controlled by members with neoliberal views who champion positions such as extreme deregulation, slashing taxes, downsizing government, and unrestricted free markets.

The reason for this is not to favor any particular political view. But rather, the reason is that the economy is already dominated by these forces. Indeed, these are the forces that caused economic inequality in the first place. These are the forces that are championed by the wealthy and the politicians they control. These are the forces that must be checked. The entire purpose of the Mend or Spend program is specifically to provide a counterweight to these prevalent forces.

The membership of the Committee, in fact, is the greatest point of vulnerability of the entire Mend or Spend program. It is a matter that will be highly contentious and will become the subject of great attacks by the wealthy and powerful entrenched interests opposed to the Mend or Spend program. It must therefore be protected zealously. If the wealthy succeed in controlling the Committee and packing it with their own agents, then the entire program could be undermined and rendered useless. The fox will have succeeded in being appointed to guard the henhouse.

Fortunately, somewhat of a check is built into the program to counter the effects of a corrupted Committee. The "Spend" component is triggered automatically if objective financial targets are not met within a specified period of time. This provides a powerful incentive for the Committee to devise measures that would actually work. It would do no good for corrupt members to deviously devise weak solutions designed to protect the wealth of the top 1% because when those weak solutions fail, the "Spend" component would be activated. So even traitorous members planted on the Committee by the wealthy would be incentivized to create solutions that would actually solve economic inequality. Nevertheless, a corrupt Committee could still undermine the program, such as by establishing weak financial targets in the first place to ensure that the "Spend" component would never be triggered.

The process for appointing members to the Committee can help to ensure their integrity, but by no means will it be infallible. The members should be appointed by the president, instead of by Congress, and should serve at the pleasure of the president. This will ensure a greater level of accountability directly to the voters. During elections, presidential candidates should be pressed by voters to issue a slate of names from which they would select the Committee members. This way, each candidate for office can be assessed on whether they are serious about supporting a strong Mend or Spend program. And if economic inequality does not improve during a presidential term, this would serve as a basis for voters to elect a different president.

Oversight of the Committee would be conducted primarily by the executive branch with additional oversight by Congress, similar to other agencies within the executive branch.

Chapter

10

A Market-Based Remedy

Regardless of whether one believes that the free market creates glorious wealth or imposes dreadful misery, virtually everyone agrees that the free market is an extraordinarily powerful tool.

Mend or Spend seeks to capture this lightning in a bottle and put it to good use.

10.1   Size Matters: Big Problem, Big Solution

Even though the problem of economic inequality seems too big to solve, Mend or Spend rises to the challenge and provides a solution equal to the task.

At first blush, Mend or Spend might appear to resort to a solution of "soaking the rich." To a certain extent, there is some truth to this notion. If the wealthy were to forego their opportunity to "Mend" and instead opted to "Spend," then the solution would take the form of taxing the rich to fund programs that help the middle class and below.

But in fact, the basis of Mend or Spend is deeper than just "soaking the rich." The magic of Mend or Spend is that it harnesses the enormous power of the free market and unleashes it upon the problem of economic inequality.

The main obstacle has been that the problem is simply too big and too diffuse. Just about every company throughout the nation has some sort of incentive to exploit its workers. Countless CEOs and boardrooms are continuously devising devious new measures to divert money away from the workers and into the hands of the shareholders.

Politicians and regulators cannot possibly prevent all of these pernicious measures because they cannot be inside all the CEO office suites and corporate boardrooms across the nation all at once. And even if the politicians solved one problem, the corporate executives would simply devise new measures to circumvent the latest regulation.

The extent of economic inequality is almost too enormous to fathom. It is the mother of all problems.

Mend or Spend, however, solves this entire mess in a single stroke. The solution is quite simple in concept.

The approach recognizes that economic inequality is not one single problem, but instead, the culprit is countless problems that exist all throughout the marketplace. Each one of these problems cannot possibly be solved on an individual basis because they are too numerous. Trying to address each instance would be a fool's errand and would amount to the world's largest game of whack-a-mole.

Instead of attempting to correct each violation and every new measure deviously devised by devilish corporations, the question becomes, what is causing all of these individual problems in the first place?

The answer to this question is readily apparent: economic incentives of the free market.

As Adam Smith explained in his seminal 1776 book, "The Wealth of Nations," the "butcher, brewer, and baker" could earn profits for themselves by producing meat, beer, and bread, and this in turn would benefit the entire community. Such a beautiful thing.

Corporate CEOs of our modern day applied this same profit-making principle. They realized that they could earn profits for themselves by taking money away from their workers. Unfortunately, however, the consequences of this profitable activity would not benefit the entire community but instead would plague the community with devastating economic inequality. Not such a beautiful thing. Yet this is the reality of how the free market operates.

Economic incentives are powerful tools. This one little incentive, namely, that CEOs and shareholders could enrich themselves by taking money away from the workers, has rippled through the entire marketplace and created countless individual problems over and over and over again all throughout the economy. This has taken many forms, such as reduced wages, slashed benefits, shuttered factories, layoffs, and on and on. One little incentive. Many big problems.

The underlying concept of Mend or Spend is to utilize this very same power of the free market, but to turn it around and use it for good.

Mend or Spend creates a powerful economic incentive. Namely, CEOs and shareholders can earn more money for themselves by solving economic inequality instead of by perpetuating it.

The new incentive is delivered through the tax code by increasing taxes on the wealthy if they fail to alleviate economic inequality.

The wealthy might contend that utilizing the tax code is not a market-based solution. But do not let them get away with this. The tax code is commonly used as a tool to encourage desired activity and discourage undesired activity. In fact, one prime example is a tax provision that is near and dear to the wealthy. Namely, the capital gains tax rate.

Why in the world should income from investments (capital gains) be taxed at a lower rate than income from wages earned in a job?

And this difference is enormous. In recent years, the highest tax rate for ordinary income has been around 40%, but for capital gains it has been only 20%. That is half as much!

This is a huge tax give-away to the rich. After all, the rich earn their income primarily from investments, whereas workers earn their income primarily from wages. The result is that the rich are taxed half as much as workers. Or, in other words, workers pay twice as much in taxes as the rich. This is the case despite the fact that the rich can easily afford to contribute a greater share toward taxes than the workers. This is upside down. Backwards. It makes a mockery of our "progressive" tax code in which higher tax rates are supposed to apply to higher incomes.

The wealthy justify this absurdity on the grounds that it provides a positive market-based incentive. They maintain that a lower tax rate on capital gains encourages greater investment, which in turn leads to the creation of more jobs, which in turn benefits the middle class.

This argument, of course, is full of fault. It seems quite obvious that handing out money from the public treasury to rich people on the mere hope that they might possibly one day spend it on something that is really terrific for the rest of us is hardly the best use of such funds, to say the least. And yet we never seem to learn our lesson when the wealthy naturally spend their tax gift primarily on themselves by buying more mansions and yachts instead of investing in society.

Furthermore, if capital gains were taxed at the same 40% rate as ordinary income, what would the wealthy do with their surplus money? Not invest? Stick it under their mattresses?

No. Of course not. They would still make the same investments.

If an investment opportunity promised to return a pre-tax profit of $10 million, an investor would still make this investment regardless of whether their after-tax profit would equal $8 million under a 20% tax rate, or $6 million under a 40% tax rate.

By not investing at all, the investor would forego the $6 million entirely and instead earn zero. So of course the investor would still make the same investment regardless of whether it returned $8 million or $6 million. Both amounts constitute a handsome profit. The only difference is that under the second scenario this rich investor would contribute a fairer share of taxes to society. That's all.

Regardless, this example of a lower tax rate being applied to capital gains makes plain that the tax code is commonly used as a tool to incentivize certain activity.

Mend or Spend is no different.

Plus, Mend or Spend is in fact a market-based approach in that it leaves entirely to the market the ability to devise its own solutions for how to go about reducing economic inequality. Indeed, under the "Mend" component, the market is given the opportunity to solve the problem completely on its own without the intervention under the "Spend" component.

Once Mend or Spend is implemented and the proper incentives under Mend or Spend are set loose in the marketplace, the effects of these incentives will ripple all throughout the economy, from big companies to small, from CEO suites to boardrooms, giving rise to an endless amount of solutions all across the nation. One solution after the next, innovation after innovation, in company after company. Market forces will be mobilized. In order to maximize their own profits (by preventing the "Spend" tax rate from being triggered), CEOs and shareholders will devise all sorts of measures for sharing more wealth with the workers, from higher salaries, to enhanced benefits, to flexible work-life arrangements, and beyond. One little incentive. Many big solutions.

For years and years, the cheerleaders of capitalism have been defending the huge pay-outs to CEOs and entrepreneurs as being fair and appropriate compensation for such extraordinary talent and brilliance. Terrific! Now all of these super-star problem-solvers can apply their phenomenal abilities to solving economic inequality.

This will be wonderful. We are so glad to have them on our team. We cannot wait to see their marvelous proposals.

Of course, there is no reason for these super-star executives to complain about the higher tax rate of the "Spend" component because they could avoid this measure altogether by merely solving economic inequality under the "Mend" component. Put all those extraordinary abilities to good use. Show us your A-game. Let's see whether you are really worth all those millions of dollars.

The nation's top CEOs and entrepreneurs would suddenly apply themselves to solving economic inequality. The best and brightest would have the proper incentive to work toward benefitting everyone throughout society and serving the best interests of our country overall.

Let the free market work its magic. Under Mend or Spend, the "invisible hand" would travel throughout the entire nation as a helping hand performing good deeds for the workers and solving the overall problem of economic inequality. Adam Smith would be so proud.

This is the true power of Mend or Spend. It harnesses the forces of the free market and applies them to solving economic inequality.

Mend or Spend is the mother of all solutions.

10.2   Counterweight to Corporate Power

One of the primary causes of economic inequality is the imbalance of power between corporations and their workers. All the power rests with the corporations.

Over the past few decades, corporations have been increasingly siphoning money away from their workers. Blow after blow have been visited upon the workers. Wages have stagnated, healthcare benefits have been reduced, 401k contribution plans have been canceled, pension plans have been eliminated, the workforce has been reduced, hours have increased, jobs have been shipped overseas under globalization, and lay-offs have taken hold.

What can the workers do in response?

Nothing. Simply nothing.

The conventional market theory is that workers could always quit their jobs and seek new employment elsewhere.

But this is highly unrealistic. First of all, it is no easy matter for workers to simply quit their jobs. Quitting a job can be a traumatic life event. Workers cannot do without a paycheck. By quitting their job, they do not know whether they could obtain a new job. And trying to conduct a job-search while maintaining an existing job can be extremely difficult, especially given the extraordinary strains of modern life of working all the time while also managing the demands of family life at home.

But further, quitting one employer will not help one bit when all the other employers in the marketplace engage in the same harmful practices.

So despite the conventional wisdom, quitting is not a viable solution. The workers have no alternatives.

The workers are essentially powerless. They have no leverage. They often cannot strike against the company because they are not organized and cannot bargain collectively. Corporations have waged a systematic campaign over many years to dismantle labor unions. This has been accomplished in part by corporations capturing politicians through campaign contributions and lobbying crusades. These politicians then dutifully served their corporate masters by enacting laws that restricted labor unions and favored corporations over workers.

Workers are left with nowhere to turn for help. They are stuck. So year after year workers have been forced to sit idly by and watch their wages stagnate, their benefits disappear, and their financial security slip away.

And all the while corporations have grown richer and richer. Nothing stands in the way of corporations wielding their inordinate bargaining power to squeeze ever more money out of the workers. There is no check on corporate power. There are no market forces to restrain corporations from abusing their dominance by extracting too much money from the workers.

Mend or Spend changes this power imbalance. Mend or Spends provides a counterweight to help offset the power of the corporations. Mend or Spend serves as a potent force in favor of the workers that counteracts the immensity of the corporations.

Under Mend or Spend, the owners and executives of corporations would suddenly have a powerful incentive to be sure that they are adequately providing for their workers. Corporations would know that they must share a greater portion of their profits with the workers or else the higher tax rate would be triggered under the "Spend" component of Mend or Spend.

Corporations would suddenly have a check on their power. They would no longer be able to mercilessly squeeze every last drop out of their workers. CEOs would know that if they pushed too hard and extracted too many pounds of flesh, they would be hit with the higher tax of the "Spend" component.

This safeguard would become a permanent element in the economy and would operate continuously into the future keeping corporate power in check and maintaining a degree of balance in the system.

Mend or Spend would function as an 800-pound gorilla constantly present in every CEO office suite and every corporate boardroom deterring exploitation and protecting the workers.

Perhaps the "invisible hand" could use a little help from an invisible gorilla.

Mend or Spend would serve as an effective counterweight to corporate dominance and would impose and maintain a certain balance of power between corporations and workers.

10.3   Draw Them to the Negotiating Table

In any negotiation, a party that possesses disproportionate power has little incentive to negotiate seriously or to make substantial concessions.

Think for example about Corporate America negotiating against their workers. The power imbalance is stark. Corporations naturally seek to extract as much profit as possible for themselves even though they know they could easily afford to share far more with their workers. They do not voluntarily make concessions to their workers. Why would they? To do so would run counter to the tenets of business.

Negotiating against the wealthy for a solution to economic inequality presents similar issues. The wealthy have no incentive to negotiate seriously, if at all. They are not under pressure to make concessions. They are free to squeeze as much as possible out of the middle class and poor to benefit themselves. And they know they can get away with it. When given the choice between helping ordinary people or increasing their own profits, the wealthy are incentivized to increase their own profits.

Mend or Spend changes this dynamic. When faced with hard deadlines and stiff penalties, suddenly the wealthy would have a powerful incentive to negotiate seriously. They would have a reason to come forward, set aside their bluffing, and offer all sorts of concessions they could well afford. They would be incentivized to come to the negotiating table and participate earnestly.

Maybe they would admit that they really did not need to cancel employee pension plans after all. Maybe they would confess that they could in fact support healthcare for all. Maybe they would concede that they could afford to pay higher wages. Much higher.

Whereas previously the wealthy appeared to have no suggestions whatsoever for how to solve economic inequality, suddenly the wealthy would emerge from the shadows and offer a veritable cornucopia of helpful ideas.

The incentives under Mend or Spend would inspire the wealthy to be more honest about their ability to cooperate with the rest of society.

10.4   Balanced Capitalism

Under a system of capitalism, the financial incentives can be perverse. The rich are often incentivized to exploit the middle class and the poor.

Mend or Spend, however, counteracts this imbalance. And it does so by working within the existing system of capitalism.

Mend or Spend utilizes the very same free-market forces that drive capitalism itself. It creates a market-based incentive for the rich to share more of their wealth with the middle class and below.

Mend or Spend functions as a balancing force. When society becomes misaligned as a result of the rich inevitably extracting too much wealth for themselves, Mend or Spend provides a financial incentive for the rich to shift some of their excess wealth back to the middle class and below. This serves to rebalance the economic distribution among the classes to maintain a more equitable proportion throughout society.

This may sound familiar. It is indeed consistent with Aristotle's solution for maintaining a viable state. Aristotle believed that a large and healthy middle class is essential to the very existence of a society. To achieve this, the wealthy must share a portion of their wealth with the people below them.

Mend or Spend accomplishes this vision. It provides the economic incentive for the rich to share their wealth. This nourishes the middle class. It results in a more equitable balance among all the classes, and thereby achieves an overall balance for society as a whole.

Mend or Spend accomplishes this by utilizing a market-based approach under capitalism without resorting to socialism or communism. Instead, Mend or Spend helps to create a more equitable system of "balanced capitalism."

Chapter

11

Fantasy or Reality?

Is Mend or Spend just a pipe dream? Pie in the sky? A glorious fantasy? Or could Mend or Spend actually be enacted?

Absolutely! This is real.

But making it happen will not be a leisurely stroll through the park. It will indeed face enormous opposition and will require determined fortitude.

11.1   Super Bowl of Corporate Lobbying

The wealthy and powerful entrenched interests that benefit from the current system of economic inequality will not simply accept this new initiative lying down. Not a chance.

Instead, they will mount a fierce opposition campaign the likes of which we have never before seen. Their mobilization will be astonishing. Their power will seem enormous. Their attacks will be ferocious.

The wealthiest people in the nation will join forces with the largest corporations in the world. They will open their personal checkbooks and corporate coffers and spend like there is no tomorrow. This is no surprise. They are facing a potential 90 percent tax rate. So in theory, they would spend up to 90 percent of their income to stop it. Billions and billions of dollars will be dedicated to defeating Mend or Spend.

The two major political parties, Republicans and Democrats, will both oppose Mend or Spend. It is hard to imagine the two polarized parties actually agreeing on anything, but when it comes to Mend or Spend, they will lock arms in solidarity against it. They will suddenly appear to be the best of friends. This is because the wealthy have infiltrated both political parties and largely control them both. So when the wealthy start buying politicians to oppose the program, they will pay-off both Republicans and Democrats alike.

Brace for a spectacle. This will give rise to the Super Bowl of lobbying. Money will pour into Washington, D.C. The wealthy will funnel limitless cash to all sorts of lobbyists and advocacy groups, much of it dark money that cannot be traced back to the original contributors. The swamp will swell into an ocean.

The wealthy will fund all sorts of political candidates throughout the nation from both parties who will suddenly pop-up out of nowhere for the purpose of running against Mend or Spend. Television and radio will be jammed with political advertisements attacking the proposal and personally trashing those who support it.

It will be an entertainment extravaganza. The circus of the swamp.

11.2 Power of the People: Unification

In the face of such powerful opposition, does Mend or Spend even stand a chance?

Yes!

In fact, the odds are in our favor.

Even though the wealthy are extremely powerful, they are extremely few in number. They are the 1%. We the People are the 99%.

The numbers are on our side.

Prior to this point in time, however, it is amazing to think that the wealthy were able to accumulate so much wealth and consolidate so much power into the hands of so few. It is truly astonishing.

This is especially mindboggling considering the fact that we possess the right to vote!

Think of the French Revolution in 1789. We assume that if the French peasants had possessed the right to vote, well, then, surely the revolution never would have occurred. The peasants would not have needed to take-up arms and storm the Bastille because they could have deposed the king and queen by vote instead of by guillotine.

It seems obvious to us today that if those French peasants could have voted, economic inequality never would have gotten out of hand in the first place. The aristocracy never would have been able to accumulate so much wealth at the expense of the peasants. The monarchs would have been voted out of office long before the inequality became so dire.

But in our own time, the same inequality occurred right under our noses, astonishingly, all while we possessed the right to vote. America is supposedly the greatest democracy in the world, and a democracy is supposed to prevent unfairness in society. Nevertheless, the wealthy 1% plundered society and carried away obscene riches for themselves all while the 99% enjoyed the right to vote.

How in the world were they able to pull this off?

Certainly, their tactical maneuvers exhibit their various achievements, such as controlling politicians who enacted favorable legislation, like slashing taxes for the wealthy, while simultaneously blocking reforms for the people. But this does not explain why the people accepted all of these unfair measures without overthrowing the politicians.

A credible explanation centers around the lack of unity among the population. The great masses of people are simply too large, divergent, and fractured to organize effectively and thus we cannot coalesce around any single issue. So even though the people possess the ultimate power of great numbers, we are incapable of harnessing our own power because we can never join together and unify.

The wealthy have long recognized this vulnerability and have shrewdly sought to exploit it. Indeed, perhaps the greatest fear of the 1% is the unification of the 99%.

So how have the wealthy been able to prevent the 99% from marching against the 1%?

Throughout history, one favorite technique employed by tyrants is the use of force to brutally suppress their own people. This still occurs today in many countries around the world. Those who dare to attempt to organize others in resistance are met with gruesome fates. They are vilified, persecuted, disappeared, imprisoned, tortured, mutilated, and murdered. This violence is specifically intended to serve as an example to everyone else that they had better think twice before organizing against the powerful at the top. It is a form of terrorism. And it can be very effective. Murdering only a few people can impose a powerful deterrent effect on the many.

But pure force is no guarantee that the population will be subdued. Force can work only if the people are sufficiently frightened into ending their resistance. If the people remain undeterred, however, then force is not an adequate protection. No army could resist 99% of the population.

While applying force is an important tool for those in power, it is not ideal. It is messy. And it creates problems of its own. Force attracts attention and scrutiny. And force instills anger and resentment throughout the population. Instead of suppressing discontent, it could backfire to produce the opposite effect of inciting discontent.

The ruling elite would much prefer a solution of suppressing the population without having to resort to force. So they devised an elegant solution.

If the 99% are not unified, then they cannot march against the 1%. The key to suppressing the population, therefore, is to prevent unification. The best way to prevent the 99% from unifying *with* each other is to keep them fighting *against* each other.

So the ruling elite sought to sow seeds of discontent among their own population. The objective is to turn people against people.

The first step is to divide the population into smaller groups. Divide and conquer. It is a simple strategy. Yet it is surprisingly effective.

Divisions can be created along numerous different fault lines. Pitting political parties against each other is a favorite. Republicans against Democrats. Religion is always a fine target. Race is another good one. Gender works well, like the role of women in society. Regional differences can be exploited. Hot-button political issues also serve the cause, from age-old standards like big government versus small government, to contemporary issues like regulating the internet.

Once the smaller groups have been identified, the next step is to foment discontent between them. Get them all riled up against each other. Vilify one particular group or another. Instill fear of one against the other. Create a sense of impending threat. Foster anger, resentment, and hate.

Eventually, each group will perceive their main opposing group as being their biggest enemy. They will oppose each other so vehemently that they could never imagine joining hands to work together across these lines of division for any reason whatsoever. They could never work with their sworn enemies. A Republican working with a Democrat? Never!

This is music to the ears of the wealthy elite. As long as these smaller groups remain divided against each other, they will never join forces with each other to oppose the 1%.

Each group will also perceive their main opposing group as being their most immediate threat and their primary problem in life. They become preoccupied with the battles between themselves. This benefits the wealthy elite because it creates a diversion. The smaller groups are so consumed by their own battles that their attention is diverted away from their true and most damaging enemy of the 1%.

Mission accomplished. The 99% are not able to unite to oppose the 1%.

This enables the wealthy elite to act under a cover of invisibility. While the attention of the smaller groups is trained upon each other, the wealthy elite are able to perpetrate their most harmful policies throughout society without attracting attention.

Keeping the population divided and fighting against each other redounds to the benefit of the wealthy few at the top. It is a method for retaining their power, control, and wealth.

One example from history of divide and conquer occurred in the south during the period of Reconstruction after the Civil War. Poor whites had strong economic incentives to join ranks with the newly freed black slaves to loosen the grip of power maintained by the ruling plantation owners. Naturally, the plantation owners sought to prevent this unification. They did so along racial lines of seeking to keep poor whites and blacks apart by turning them against each other. The ruling elite disseminated information portraying black people as inferior and as posing a dangerous threat to poor white people.

The strategy worked. Racial integration was not achieved in the south during and after Reconstruction. And poverty among blacks and whites alike remained a persistent problem despite the fact that their joining together would have given them greater political power.

In the present day, numerous divisions exist among the 99%. Just think of some of the hot-button issues, like abortion, religious freedom, racial discrimination, gay rights, immigration, gun control, and the divide between sparsely populated rural areas and densely populated urban areas.

Many of these issues are encompassed by the great polarization between the two main political parties. The nation is divided between Republicans and Democrats, and the two parties increasingly despise one another. Both parties are preoccupied with constant battles on every issue and with fighting against the other.

All of this division clearly benefits the wealthy. Divide and conquer.

As long as the 99% remain divided, the 1% will conquer.

Aha!

From our weakness we find our strength.

We must get smart. Wake up. Snap to.

Right before our very eyes is the roadmap for the solution.

The key to success for Mend or Spend lies in the ability to unify the 99%.

Unification. This is all it takes. The wealthy 1% can deploy all the money in the world against Mend or Spend, but when the 99% are united, all of that money is rendered worthless.

The 99% can actually unify to support Mend or Spend. The reason is that the only divide on this issue is the 99% on one side and the 1% on the other. There are no other contentious issues that would threaten to divide the 99% against ourselves.

Mend or Spend is genuinely non-partisan. Many issues claim to be non-partisan when in truth they are not. But Mend or Spend actually is purely non-partisan. Both Republicans and Democrats within the 99% will support it because they all benefit equally. Independent voters will support it as well for the same reason.

Mend or Spend cuts through all the divisive issues of identity politics to appeal universally to everyone. Men and women. Young and old. Black, white, Latino, Asian, Middle Eastern, you name it. Everyone benefits equally.

And the same is true with cultural issues. Differences disappear and everyone finds themselves on the same side. Religious and secular. Pro-life and pro-choice. Straight and gay. Urban and rural. Pro-gun and pro-gun control. Christian, Jewish, Muslim, Hindu, Buddhist, none of the above, or other. It doesn't matter.

Everyone in the 99% economic group will support Mend or Spend.

Economic inequality can be solved. The 99% can join together and prevail over the 1%.

Power to the people!

11.3   Electrify the Electorate

Mend or Spend will thrill voters all across the nation and inspire people to turn out to the polls.

Although it may seem surprising, many citizens in the United States do not exercise their right to vote.

On the surface, this appears to be tragic. After all, possessing the right to vote is an extraordinary privilege. Just think of all the people in other countries around the world who are deprived of the right to vote and who suffer horrendous oppression as a result. And think of all the struggle and sacrifice that our forbearers endured in the United States just to obtain the right to vote. It took an entire revolutionary war, and a women's suffrage movement, and a civil rights movement. Yet many American citizens today squander this precious right by not voting at all. It seems inconceivable.

Upon deeper consideration, however, a rational explanation becomes apparent.

The right to vote offers power only to the extent that citizens are able to vote on issues that are meaningful.

Yet somehow our elections do not seem to offer meaningful choices.

In election after election, there are seldom any outstanding candidates on the ballot and almost never any meaningful issues at stake. Of course, there are occasional exceptions, and sometimes even significant exceptions, but for the most part, it's blah blah blah, ho hum, same old same old.

The candidates, underneath their facades, are virtually indistinguishable in substance. Sure, they may present themselves as diametrically opposed, and they may sling insults at one another over inflammatory issues that create the illusion of presenting voters with a monumental choice. But on issues that genuinely matter, they are not very different at all.

And what are the issues that genuinely matter? Well, we simply do not know. Important issues are not discussed. In fact, they are not even presented to the voters. Out of sight, out of mind.

This is no accident.

Both political parties are controlled by the wealthy. And the wealthy of course desire that candidates remain silent about issues pertaining to the inordinate power of the top 1%. You betcha. The name of the game is to keep their power hidden out of view from the population. So aspiring political candidates cannot rise through the ranks in either party unless they play the game and avoid raising the important issues.

This is not to suggest the existence of any sort of grand conspiracy wherein a small group of super-rich people meet a few times a year in a secret location and decide the fate of the world. No. It does not happen that way. Instead, it happens as a natural consequence of wealthy people simply pursuing their own financial interests. There is no need for any secret meeting of the super-rich because they act in unison anyway to protect their interests, such as by funding political candidates who do not threaten their own wealth and power.

By the time aspiring politicians become actual candidates for office, they all share the same political views when it comes to protecting and hiding the wealth and power of the rich. There is no divergence among the candidates, regardless of party. Both the Democrats and the Republicans are beholden to the wealthy. So the campaigns contain little or no discussion about the enormous power of the 1%. And there is hardly ever any opposition to the interests of the wealthy. The candidates by this point are highly skilled at avoiding any such matters.

The party machines have long understood the ploy of controlling candidates in order to control elections. A poignant quote captures this point, attributed to William "Boss" Tweed, a state senator in New York and the head of Tammany Hall, a corrupt political machine that dominated New York during the latter half of the 1800s. Boss Tweed purportedly remarked, "I don't care who does the electing, so long as I get to do the nominating."

It's an old trick. An oldie but a goodie.

The mainstream media are complicit in all of this. They focus on issues that create conflict between candidates. They are obsessed with covering conflict since this is the way to boost ratings in a viciously competitive media business. They do not waste their resources pursuing issues on which all candidates agree.

Tellingly, almost all of the mainstream media outlets are themselves owned or controlled by wealthy corporations or individuals. So the media are hopelessly conflicted. They have a strong disincentive against pursuing issues that challenge the domination of their owners. And for good reason.

The owners would hardly allow their media companies to highlight issues that threaten the power of the owners. Journalists who wish to succeed in their careers know better than to rock the boat with these sorts of issues. These are the journalists who are rewarded with better and better assignments and promoted up through the ranks.

So candidates in elections do not even introduce important issues that are meaningful to the people. We seldom hear about corporate domination, the corruption of politicians by the wealthy, or the inordinate power of the wealthy in our society. These issues should be the banner headlines on the front pages of newspapers and the lead stories on television newscasts. But they are not. Instead, when they appear at all, they are relegated to the back pages.

To be sure, there are many outstanding journalists and writers. Our free press is the lifeblood of our democracy, and journalists are often the unsung heroes of our freedoms. But nonetheless, despite multiple 24-hour cable news networks and a plethora of print and online news outlets, it remains extremely difficult for an ordinary citizen to understand the essence of our society's issues.

Elections are duly held on a regular basis. Citizens enjoy the right to vote. The ritual of going to the polling station and casting the ballot in the voting booth makes us feel that we live in a democracy and that we possess the power to determine the direction of our society. It seems wonderful.

But it all distracts us away from realizing that the candidates running in the elections are not the sort of people we desire as our leaders. The issues presented in the elections are not the issues that we wish we could decide. Our votes, weirdly, do not give us the ability to address the most pressing problems in our society.

Even though the people have the power of the vote, the vote has little power.

It is quite a phenomenon, actually. Citizens possess the right to vote, yet simultaneously, these votes do not change society.

Remarkably, the citizens do not seem to notice this astonishing disparity. We all keep voting, election after election, but society never changes as a result. The problems of ordinary people are never addressed. The fundamental unfairness in society is never improved.

It is an astonishing feat. Despite the fact that the 99% possess the power to vote, the top 1% have managed to surreptitiously slide the real power out from under the population all while keeping in place the elaborate system of the democratic right to vote.

Voting has been reduced to a grand illusion. With great fanfare, citizens are taught that they possess the solemn responsibility of voting. They are instilled with the conviction that they hold in their hands the great power to shape society. They are made to believe that they alone possess the power to determine their own fate.

But of course it is a deception. A façade. A false pretense.

Voting itself has become a mere ritual that is little more than a charade.

In reality, the vote has been divested of its power. Defanged. Neutralized.

If we are not able to vote for anything meaningful, then our vote has no meaning.

People have come to understand this reality intuitively. In the past we have voted time and again with great optimism only to discover that no positive change ever results.

Through the bitter reality of experience, people have come to realize that their vote will make no difference. Their vote will not change anything. Their vote will not improve their circumstances.

So it is no wonder that many citizens do not vote. They feel powerless. They know they are not able to vote on important issues that will change their lives. They know their vote will not matter.

Mend or Spend changes all this.

For the first time, people will have the opportunity to vote on something that really matters. Something that will make a difference to them personally. Something that will change their lives.

Mend or Spend enables people to directly vote on economic inequality. They can vote "yes" to solving this problem. They can vote in favor of economic justice. They can vote to improve their own financial situation.

People will recognize that Mend or Spend fundamentally alters the power dynamic. The top 1% would be forced to actually help the 99%. Power would suddenly be shifted to the people down below. Each voter knows that their single vote is needed to empower the people as a whole. Each voter knows that they are important to the cause. Each voter knows that their vote will make a difference.

People will understand that Mend or Spend addresses an issue larger than themselves. It seeks to achieve greater fairness throughout society. People will recognize the significance of this ideal. They will be inspired by its inherent goodness. And they will feel passionate about being a part of this phenomenon by casting their votes in solidarity with the movement.

For the first time, We the People of the 99% will be given real power in an election. We will realize that this vote can improve our own lives. We will understand that this vote can bring greater fairness to society.

We will know that, this time, our vote will matter.

11.4   Threshold Campaign Issue

When Mend or Spend becomes a campaign issue during elections, all the other divisive political issues, unfortunately, will not magically disappear. These other contentious issues will remain front and center in the same elections along with Mend or Spend. This leads to the potential problem that Mend or Spend could become lost in the jumble of all the other issues and fade away into obscurity.

To prevent this, voters must treat Mend or Spend as a threshold issue in every campaign. The first question posed to every candidate, regardless of party, must be whether they support Mend or Spend. This will become a qualifying question. If a candidate does not support Mend or Spend, then voters must reject them immediately. No need to hear another word about any of their other positions. They are done.

For candidates who do support Mend or Spend, they "pass go" and can proceed to the regular food-fight over all the other contentious political issues of the day.

By making Mend or Spend a threshold issue, every viable candidate in every race would support Mend or Spend. Republican, Democrat, and Independent. Everyone. It would not even be an election issue because all candidates would universally support it. The elections would instead turn on the contentious political issues of the day, just like any other election.

In this case, when the election has ended, regardless of the winning party and candidate, Mend or Spend would be supported.

This effectively turns Mend or Spend into a so-called "litmus test." Imposing a litmus test is almost always a bad idea because candidates who are otherwise highly attractive can be knocked out of contention due only to a single issue. But Mend or Spend is a rare exception. A litmus test is justified in this case because Mend or Spend addresses such an enormous problem plaguing society and 99% of the population favor it.

The litmus test would not knock-out otherwise good candidates. If a candidate refused to support Mend or Spend, then they would not be supporting the people and thus would not be a good candidate. Plus, due to the popularity of Mend or Spend, it would be easy to field another candidate with equivalent positions but who supported Mend or Spend.

11.5 Single-Bullet Solution

An enormous barrier to solving economic inequality has been its complexity.

If solving economic inequality could be reduced to a single check-the-box question on a ballot, like "Yes, solve inequality" or "No, do not solve inequality," then the entire 99% would vote to solve it.

The reality, however, is that no single measure could possibly solve the problem. It is simply too big. Any solution would consist of a complex set of multiple programs, such as changes to the tax code, labor laws, educational system, healthcare system, and financial system, to name a few.

It would be inconceivable to present a full set of complex policy proposals to the voters in an election. It would be overwhelming and much too detailed. People cannot be expected to suddenly become experts in multiple disciplines in order to evaluate this level of technical intricacy.

Also, the over-complexity of introducing numerous different policy proposals would threaten the viability of enacting an overall solution. Each individual component would be debated endlessly with supporters and detractors on both sides and would thereby ensure that nothing would ever be enacted.

Mend or Spend solves the problem of over-complexity. It wraps all the components into a single overall proposal that can be effectively presented to the voters. It lends itself to clear and concise messaging in campaigns. Mend or Spend will become a simple referendum on the single issue of whether to solve economic inequality for the middle class and below. It comes as close as possible to reducing the issue down to a simple vote of "yes" or "no."

Chapter

12

Class Warfare

The wealthy will allege that Mend or Spend is class warfare. They will warn in apocalyptic terms that the dangers of class warfare will lay ruin to our cherished society.

To be sure, they are correct about the dangers of class warfare. Indeed, pitting economic classes against each other ordinarily is a profoundly bad idea. It foments anger and resentment among citizens, creates divisiveness throughout society, and leads to disaster.

The French Revolution (1789-1799) serves as the master lesson. When the peasants rose up and overthrew the monarchy, this did not suddenly produce a wonderful society of peace and harmony. No. The revolution led to decades of horrendous strife, murder, and war.

When the peasants took power, they unleashed a wave of vengeance of atrocious violence and beheadings that became known as the "Reign of Terror." Those who suffered the fate of the guillotine were not limited to just the villains in the aristocracy, but eventually included all sorts of innocent people like political dissidents who merely disagreed with the views of those in power. The rule of the peasants spun out of control and became a tyranny itself.

The violence spread to other countries as well and caused the French Revolutionary Wars (1792-1802) and the Napoleonic Wars (1803-1815) of France against other European nations. By the time Napoleon was defeated at Waterloo in 1815, it had been some 25 years after the peasants had first risen up to begin the French Revolution, at a cost of millions of deaths and untold destruction.

Indeed, class warfare *is* dangerous.

With respect to Mend or Spend, however, beware of sophistry peddled by the wealthy elite.

By denigrating Mend or Spend as class warfare, the wealthy will attempt to brand Mend or Spend as the instigator and the cause of the problem. Watch out for this little trick.

This is the equivalent of blaming the peasants for causing the French Revolution. After all, it was the peasants who rose up. If they would have just remained in their villages and kept quiet, everything would have been fine.

But the peasants were not the cause. The peasants were the reaction.

The reason the peasants rose up was not because they were overjoyed with happiness in their lives. It was not because they wanted to celebrate their delight. It was not because they had so much excess leisure time and had nothing better to do. No.

The peasants rose up as a result of their dire economic condition. They were suffering from tremendous depravity and economic oppression at the hands of the wealthy aristocracy. The peasants were compelled to take extreme measures by the severe unfairness imposed upon them.

The same is true with Mend or Spend. It is a reaction. A corrective measure. A defensive response.

Like in the French Revolution, the cause of the problem today is the drastic economic inequality that plagues our society. This unfairness has been inflicted upon the people by the wealthy elite at the top.

Class warfare is already underway. It was started by the wealthy.

Mend or Spend is merely the response by the common people to defend themselves against the attack.

The wealthy started the class warfare.

Mend or Spend will end it.

Chapter

13

Too Tough on the Wealthy?

Is Mend or Spend too tough on the wealthy?

Truth be told, Mend or Spend is no picnic for the wealthy. It does indeed impose a degree of coercion. This is not ideal because our free society is generally averse to imposing force upon individuals. Even though the force in this case is applied entirely in the form of economic incentives and not through physical force, it is a form of force nonetheless.

The wealthy will no doubt feel compelled into acting against their desire. They will not wish to "Mend" by helping to create programs designed to reduce their own wealth. Nor will they wish to "Spend" by contributing a whopping 90 percent of their income under a new tax. Yet they have no alternative. So they will feel a sense of coercion.

13.1   A Problem of Their Own Making

Before we shed too many tears for the wealthy, let us remember why they are being enlisted as a source for the solution. The reason is that it is the wealthy who caused the problem in the first place.

Although the wealthy may feel coerced now, they showed little concern about coercing others in the past. If anyone is entitled to feel coerced, surely it is the middle class and the poor. These are the people who have been suffering economic hardship for decades. They have been forced to toil away endlessly in unfulfilling jobs for insufficient wages while the wealthy enjoyed extraordinary freedom.

It is the wealthy who enriched themselves through this system of economic inequality. The wealthy did not show much concern for the masses of humanity who were forced to struggle on meager wages while the wealthy enjoyed a level of opulence beyond imagination. And at every turn, the wealthy blocked attempts at reasonable reform.

The wealthy will no doubt wail against the higher taxes of Mend or Spend by saying something like, "Why do you wish to punish us for our success?"

This, of course, is absurd.

This sort of argument seeks to turn reality on its head by portraying the wealthy as innocent victims who are being unfairly persecuted. Nothing could be further from the truth.

Sharing a portion of their obscene overabundance of wealth with those who are suffering with none is hardly a punishment. Indeed, the middle class and below are the ones who have been punished by working hard and playing by the rules yet having the promise of financial security pulled out from under them.

Accumulating vast riches for oneself by shifting income away from the middle class and the poor is hardly the type of "success" that society should reward.

Correcting these prior misdeeds to achieve a more equitable balance throughout society is hardly a punishment.

Despite past injustices, Mend or Spend seeks only fairness, not retribution. It does not mistreat the wealthy. It actually extends a high degree of consideration to the wealthy.

The program is designed to first invite the wealthy to participate voluntarily in finding a solution to economic inequality. This is reflected in the "Mend" component. No coercion is involved there. The wealthy are afforded the opportunity to solve the problem as they see fit and thus control their own fate. If they are able to voluntarily solve economic inequality, then force is never applied and the "Spend" component never takes effect.

13.2   Makers and Takers

Some among the wealthy will feel a sense of indignation at how the common people could possibly be so ungrateful for all the wonderful contributions to society made by the wealthy. According to them, the wealthy are the "makers," whereas the people are the "takers."

The "makers" invent new products, start companies, and create jobs. The "takers" are mere grubbers out for a paycheck every week without contributing very much, or worse, they draw government benefits subsidized by others.

There is a kernel of truth to this view. We do indeed desire a society that is a meritocracy in which the best and brightest can rise through the ranks to the top based purely upon their individual abilities and hard work. We do indeed want our best and brightest to invent products, start companies, and create jobs. And we are willing to reward them handsomely for their contributions to society.

Unfortunately, however, the system has not functioned as desired. All too often, the reality has not lived up to the propaganda. People become wealthy not by contributing to society, but by making withdrawals out of it. People get ahead not by lifting up others, but by stepping on them. The brightest use their keen intellects not to benefit the great many who are less intellectually endowed, but instead to take advantage of them. The ablest do not seek to improve the system for the benefit of everyone, but instead seek to exploit the loopholes for their own gain.

The economic system works very well in rewarding those who make it to the top. But the economic system falls woefully short in applying checks and balances to ensure that the actions receiving the rewards properly benefit others and society overall.

We entrust wealth and power to the "makers." But all too often these "makers" turn around and abuse their wealth and power by exploiting others, entrenching themselves, and serving their own interests.

The "makers," it turns out, are often the worst "takers."

13.3 Is the Tax Too High?

Wealthy critics of Mend or Spend will no doubt wail and howl that imposing such a steep tax rate upon them of, say, 90%, is crazy and will lead to the destruction of the nation.

Don't fall for it.

The truth is that for most of our modern society, taxes on the super-rich have been far higher than today. And guess what? Society was much more fair for everyone with far less economic inequality.

Dating all the way back to the first introduction of the federal income tax in 1913, and extending all the way up to contemporary times in the 1980s, the top tax rate for the super wealthy averaged approximately 70%. Yes, that's right, 70%. For a period of almost seven decades! Straight!

And for many of these years the highest tax rate was even higher. From 1944 all the way up through 1963, the top marginal tax rate exceeded 90%. Yes, that's right, 90%. For twenty years straight. Imagine that.

And keep in mind that this twenty-year period included the entire decade of the great prosperity of the 1950s, and a full eight years under the Republican President Dwight Eisenhower. Furthermore, for the first two years of this twenty-year period, 1944-1945, the rate was its highest ever at 94%.

Taxing the wealthy has been a pillar of our modern era. This lasted for so many decades because it reflects the fundamental principle that the wealthy should contribute an extra share to society through enhanced tax rates on extremely high incomes. This is just basic fairness. Those who have greater amounts of excess income can well afford to contribute a greater share toward society.

So we have been here before. The nation has already experienced substantial tax rates on the wealthy, including above 90%. Did society crumble? Did the sky fall? Did the economy implode? Not even close. Our nation was just fine, thank you. In fact, it prospered.

So how did this come to an end?

Unfortunately, we failed to heed the warnings of history.

Aristotle and Plato warned us some 2,400 years ago that the wealthy will scheme and maneuver to increase their own wealth at the expense of the middle class and society as a whole. Their warnings proved to be prophetic.

This is exactly what happened in our modern time beginning in the 1980s. The wealthy managed to capture the politicians, and they used their might not to improve society overall for the benefit of everyone, but instead – surprise, surprise – to drastically slash their own taxes.

Under President Ronald Reagan beginning in 1980, the super-rich enjoyed a shockingly huge tax cut. The top tax rate for the wealthy was slashed from 70% all the way down to 28%.

This was not just a minor reduction. This was not just shaving-off a few points. This was not just a modest concession. A reduction of 5% or 10% would have been plenty. Even 20% would have been way too much. But no. This was a reduction of 60%.

It was nothing less than a bonanza.

Ever since, the wealthy have been on a mad mission to protect their jackpot and keep the highest tax rate down at this ridiculously low level. And they have been extremely successful.

President Bill Clinton was able to nudge the highest rate back up a little bit to 39.6% in 1993, but President George W. Bush dropped it back down to 35% in 2003. With great difficulty, President Barack Obama nudged the rate back up to 39.6% in 2013. But President Donald Trump came along and, resembling President Reagan, slashed it once again in 2018. Trump reduced the top rate to 37%, but under Trump's completely new and utterly baseless 20% deduction for income received from "pass-through" entities (like limited liability companies), the top rate can be as low as 29.6%. This amounts to a 25% tax cut for the super wealthy, like Trump himself.

This tax rate on the wealthy is less than half of where it has been for most of our modern history.

Such a low tax on the wealthy simply makes no sense, especially during a time when our nation is plagued with drastic economic inequality. It is welfare for the wealthy. And it is nothing less than scandalous and obscene.

The true problem is not that Mend or Spend seeks to impose taxes upon the wealthy that are far too high. Instead, the true problem is that for decades the taxes on the wealthy have been far too low.

13.4   Exodus Out of America?

In response to the proposal of Mend or Spend, we will no doubt hear endless cries that this will cause a massive "brain drain" with all of America's best and brightest rich people fleeing to foreign countries that do not tax the wealthy so heavily.

This is nonsense. First of all, rich people almost certainly would not leave. America offers the best living environment in the world, and they know it. They desire to live and raise their families right here in the United States.

But even if they did leave... Good riddance.

Let them go. If they are the sort of people who would sacrifice our society for their own selfish profit, then they do not belong in positions of wealth and power in the first place.

Furthermore, a "brain drain" would not occur. There are plenty of highly intelligent people who care about our society who would remain in America. The business assets left behind by the fleeing rich would be transferred to far more responsible people and we would all be better for it as a result.

Also, if America were to raise taxes on the rich, this would serve as a shining example to other advanced democracies in the world and they too would similarly increase taxes in their own countries. This would reverse the abominable current trend of the "race to the bottom" where countries foolishly undercut each other to poach corporate business by slashing internal tax rates. Instead, it would create a "race to the top" of one country after another improving their internal societies by solving the problem of economic inequality.

Furthermore, the international community could implement disincentives against a global race to the bottom. Any rogue nation that created a tax haven for the wealthy and thus triggered the risk of a global race to the bottom could be subjected to austere measures, such as draconian tariffs on a global basis.

Another similar complaint we will no doubt hear from the wealthy is that by taxing them so highly, they would simply stop working. They would no longer be motivated to so much as get out of bed in the morning. And this, they will say, would be a terrible result for all the rest of us because the best and the brightest people would no longer put to use their extraordinary talents for the benefit of ordinary people like us.

This, of course, is more nonsense. Highly motivated people would not just give up all activity in their lives. Many people are motivated by seeking fulfillment through dedicating themselves to meaningful work. People who are driven only by amassing riches for themselves are the sort of people we do not need anyway. We would all be better off if they did stay in bed.

If the wealthy were not constantly tempted by so many opportunities to gouge innocent people in order to acquire riches for themselves, they would not flee America or do nothing with their lives. Instead, they would miraculously transform into upstanding members of society pursuing meaningful endeavors and contributing their fair share to the good of the whole.

13.5   Tried and True: We Solved This Before

We have been down this road before. We came, we saw, we conquered economic inequality.

America once before suffered from drastic economic inequality. It occurred during the Gilded Age in the decades of the late 1800s and early 1900s. This was the era of the Industrial Revolution and the "robber barons" like Rockefeller, Vanderbilt, Carnegie, Mellon, and Morgan. Capitalism was largely unregulated and it rampaged throughout the nation creating great wealth for a select few but imposing great suffering upon the many.

Economic inequality was tearing apart the nation from within. It was a classic battle of capital versus labor with capital suppressing wages and benefits of the workers. During the twenty-five year period from 1880-1905, the nation suffered over 35,000 labor strikes. Some of them turned violent. In many instances, corporate bosses convinced politicians to deploy police forces (at taxpayer expense) on the side of the corporations and against the striking workers. Some strikes were so extensive that they triggered the deployment of the state or even the federal military, often on the side of the corporations.

Even presidents intervened in various labor strikes. President Rutherford Hayes (1877-1881) sent the National Guard to the great railroad strike of 1877. President Grover Cleveland (1885-1889, 1893-1897) used the army to break the Pullman railroad strike in 1894 that had been triggered by a reduction in worker wages. And President Theodore Roosevelt (1901-1909) mediated the labor dispute during the coal strike of 1902.

Perhaps most shocking is the degree of force used by the corporations. In the Homestead Massacre in 1892 in the area of Pittsburgh, Pennsylvania, steel workers went on strike against a steel corporation owned by the tycoon Andrew Carnegie, and the striking workers occupied the steel mill. In response, Carnegie's corporation hired a private security force of about three hundred armed soldiers from the Pinkerton security company to storm the mill. An armed battle ensued with casualties on both sides totaling around ten deaths and twenty injuries.

In the Ludlow Massacre in 1914 at Ludlow, Colorado, coal miners went on strike against their mining corporation owned by the tycoon John D. Rockefeller, Jr. About one thousand striking workers and their families set-up camp in a field and were living in tents. Private security forces hired by the corporation along with the Colorado National Guard attacked the workers and their families by firing machine guns into the defenseless camp of tents. Approximately 21 people were killed, including innocent wives and children of the miners.

This level of violence is astonishing. The owners of these corporations are among the wealthiest men in the nation. Yet when their workers dare to seek even modest wage increases, these corporate titans respond with ruthless violence. They are even willing to kill their own workers. This is especially stunning given that the workers are the people who perform all of the difficult and dangerous labor, and it is from the backs of these workers that the titans earn their vast riches.

But it does not matter. The titans show no human empathy for their own workers when it comes to the subject of enriching themselves.

The oppression of workers throughout the land for decades grew into a political movement that in the early 1900s gave rise to the Progressive Era. This produced a barrage of reforms and regulations that ended the unfairness of the Gilded Age and improved society immeasurably.

The Progressive Era finally alleviated the scourge of extreme economic inequality. This was achieved in no small measure due to the introduction of the federal income tax in 1913 by the Sixteenth Amendment to the United States Constitution.

It is difficult to imagine today, but before this, there had been no federal income tax. The robber barons were extracting their millions of dollars from society without paying any income tax whatsoever.

Introducing the income tax was no easy feat. Just imagine the challenges and opposition to creating an income tax for the very first time where one did not exist at all. It took an enormous effort that lasted over two decades, including the income tax being declared unconstitutional and struck down by the United States Supreme Court in 1895. This necessitated the constitutional amendment that finally culminated in 1913.

For most of the nation's modern history, the highest tax rate on the wealthy has been substantial, averaging around 70% for almost seven decades straight, and even climbing to over 90%. This was deemed fair and appropriate as the proper contribution from the wealthy to society. And it went a long way toward reducing economic inequality.

But then beginning in the 1980s, the wealthy captured the politicians and slashed their own taxes from 70% all the way down to 28%.

The result has been predictable. The rich have grown richer, and the middle class and the poor have been left to struggle. Since the massive tax cuts for the rich began in the

1980s, society has suffered tremendous economic inequality.

If this history offers a lesson it is plain to see. It echoes the voices of Aristotle and Plato from over two thousand years ago. We should finally learn the lesson that the wealthy cannot be trusted to care for others. They simply will not do so. Instead, they will always act to increase their own wealth even at the expense of the middle class, the poor, and society. They cannot resist riches.

As a result, the wealthy cannot be left to their own devices. They must always be closely observed and constantly scrutinized. And they must be compelled to do the right thing because they will not do so voluntarily. The power of the law must be brought to bear to prevent their destructive machinations and compel them to act in the interest of the greater good.

The solution for our current problem is clear. Just as the income tax of 1913 alleviated the economic inequality of the Gilded Age, we must increase taxes on the wealthy today in order to alleviate the economic inequality of our own time.

We did it before. We can do it again.

13.6   The Reaction Could Be Worse

The reaction against the wealthy could be far worse than just Mend or Spend.

Given the extent of economic inequality inflicted upon the middle class and poor for decades, the wealthy are getting off easy.

The alternatives are much more menacing. Instead of taxing only the income of the wealthy, a tax could be imposed upon accumulated wealth to break apart the great fortunes of the rich and distribute the treasure among the poor.

Or perhaps the consequences could extend beyond just economics. The nation could experience a rise of populism with the election of dangerous demagogues who falsely proclaim to champion the common people but who in truth are more interested in usurping tyrannical power for themselves than in preserving democracy. As democratic institutions crumbled and the nation spiraled downward into authoritarianism, the wealthy would be forced to sacrifice not only their money but also their freedoms.

Or perhaps the people could rise up, storm the estates of the wealthy, seize their property, and perpetrate acts of violence.

When the wealthy become too greedy and extract too much from society for themselves, society is threatened with ruin. This was described by Aristotle and Plato over two thousand years ago. It came to life in the French Revolution of 1789. And America itself has come dangerously close to meeting a similar fate.

President Theodore "Teddy" Roosevelt (1901-1909) was gravely concerned with just such a threat during the Gilded Age, which, like today, was plagued by drastic economic inequality.

Roosevelt was appalled at the greed and exploitation by, as he described it, the "malefactors of great wealth" who sought to avoid government oversight in order to "enjoy unmolested the fruits of their own evil-doing."

Astounding words.

Roosevelt clearly understood the dangers posed by the wealthy. This is certainly familiar because it is the same sentiment that had been expressed by Aristotle and Plato.

Curiously, Roosevelt himself had been born into wealth and privilege and was among the elite. Yet he proved to be a shining example that rich people can, in fact, rise above their own circumstance and recognize that the ruling class at the top must share their wealth with the classes down below. And if they fail to do so voluntarily, then the wealthy elite must be compelled to do so involuntarily.

In order to preserve "healthy liberty" in society, Roosevelt believed that the government must use its power to limit the wealth and influence of those at the top who had acquired it through exploiting others instead of by serving others and benefitting society.

Roosevelt put forth multiple proposals during the Progressive Era designed to rein in the wealthy and uplift the middle class and poor, including trust-busting, regulating corporations, advancing labor unions, and his Square Deal reform program.

The purpose of Roosevelt's reforms was to save American society from the wealthy predators who could not control their greed and thus were leading the nation toward violent uprisings or even into revolution.

In the aftermath of the Progressive Era, the wealthy seemed to have understood the dangers of such drastic inequality. They accepted much higher tax rates on themselves for many decades. Perhaps this was due to the fact that they lived through the horrific consequences of war. They suffered through World War I (1914-1918). And only a few years later, they must have been astonished to witness the rise of right-wing fascism in Europe, such as under Benito Mussolini in Italy in 1922, and Adolf Hitler in Germany in 1933, that plunged the world once again headlong into the devastation of World War II (1939-1945).

This must have terrified the wealthy. It may well have shaken them into seeing the unvarnished truth that an unequal society leads to horrendous consequences that are far too high to bear. So the wealthy contributed higher taxes, accepted lower salaries for themselves, and shared the wealth with the middle class. As a result, the nation enjoyed decades of prosperity during the post-war period.

But memories fade. Past lessons recede. And the tentacles of greed grow back.

By the 1980s, the world wars seemed to have receded far away into the distant past. Along came President Ronald Reagan who proudly slashed the taxes paid by the wealthy to near historic lows, from 70% all the way down to 28%. Since then, the nation has been sliding deeper and deeper into ever worsening economic inequality.

Today, our society seems to have regressed backward. We find ourselves back in the same situation we faced during the Gilded Age. If the wealthy do not wake up and solve the scourge of economic inequality, violent social rupture could very well be the result.

Like Teddy Roosevelt's reform programs, Mend or Spend would save society from the wealthy predators of today. It would also save the wealthy from none other than themselves because Mend or Spend would impose much softer consequences upon the wealthy than social strife and potentially devastating eruptions of violence.

13.7   Is Mend or Spend a Revolution?

By the modern-day standard of our government doing next to nothing to combat economic inequality, Mend or Spend indeed is a radical revolution.

But judging by the sweep of history, Mend or Spend is actually quite mild. People are not taking up arms, seizing property, and overthrowing the aristocracy.

In fact, the original act of radical violence was perpetrated not by the poor masses but by the wealthy few in creating economic inequality in the first place. Outrage by the people is indeed justified. But Mend or Spend would peacefully defuse this outrage and restore fairness in society. So in this sense, Mend or Spend is actually preventing a far more destructive revolution.

When we consider whether Mend or Spend is fair to the wealthy 1%, we must also consider the unfairness to the 99% in the absence of Mend or Spend. Under this comparison, there is no contest. The existing inequality is far too extreme to constitute a healthy society. The wealthy few at the top receive far too much and the masses of people down below receive far too little.

The fact alone that society is so unfairly stratified is proof positive that the wealthy are being overcompensated for activities that do not adequately benefit society. Indeed, if their activities benefitted society sufficiently, then drastic economic inequality would not exist because their activities would have already corrected the problem.

But, alas, for the problem has not been corrected.

We must now take it upon ourselves to balance the scales.

13.8   Vilifying the Wealthy?

Are the wealthy monsters? Are they mean and nasty ogres perfectly willing to inflict cruelty upon innocent people without caring one single bit?

Well, actually, yes, some of them are monsters. They are consumed with amassing as much money as possible for themselves and they have no concern whatsoever for the well-being of anyone else.

But not all of them are monsters. Some are good people who just so happen to be doing bad things. And often, who can blame them? After all, they are being paid a lot of money to do these bad things. And they are not being offered alternative opportunities to do good things for a similar amount of money.

The problem is not so much with diabolical behavior by individuals themselves, but rather, the larger problem is with the overall system. The incentives are upside down. If large sums of money can be earned through activities that harm society, then guess what? People will in fact engage in such activities regardless of the harm caused to society. This is not entirely their fault because they are merely following the pathway to making money for themselves. Society has guided them in this direction. It is almost unfair to expect these people to choose otherwise.

What is needed, desperately, is a realignment of incentives so people are not rewarded with large sums for exploiting society, but instead can earn large sums only by benefitting society.

The perspective of Mend or Spend is not to vilify the wealthy. Wealth in itself is not wrong. Indeed, the more wealthy people, the better. So long as basic financial security is provided to everyone is society, then individuals should be permitted to become wealthy in reward for contributions that benefit society.

Wealth becomes a problem, however, when it is earned in ways that harm other people, or when a small number of people amass great wealth for themselves while leaving behind the majority of the people in hardship.

Mend or Spend is not against wealth. It is against poverty.

13.9   Dear Wealthy: It's for Your Own Good

Even though Mend or Spend seems to harm the wealthy, in truth it actually benefits them. In the short-term, the wealthy will indeed experience a reduction in their wealth. This will be painful to them and thus they will decry Mend or Spend as harmful.

The truth, however, is that pervasive economic inequality poses a far greater threat to society overall, including to the wealthy. If we do not alter our current course, society will continue to decline.

As the middle class crumbles, so too will stability. As people are pushed out of the middle class, poverty will swell. This creates a downward spiral that triggers numerous other negative consequences that would be difficult to reverse. As jobs are lost and wages decrease, property values decline, tax revenues suffer, and community services and social investment wither. Police and fire departments are slashed, hospitals close, and homeless shelters and services for people in need disappear. Crime rises. Drug addiction rises. Law enforcement is insufficient to contain it. Criminal gangs and organized crime take hold. Entire neighborhoods fall into decline. Our society overall stratifies into two segments: the poor underclass and the wealthy upper class.

The greatest suffering, of course, is borne by the people in the underclass. But such stark stratification is also not good for the wealthy.

Even though the wealthy become richer, their lives become poorer. They are forced to build more and more gated communities with higher and higher walls that further isolate them. They find it more and more difficult to emerge from their walls into public spaces, such as shopping malls, grocery stores, restaurants, parks, public schools, and houses of worship. They increasingly become targets of crime, including serious crimes like kidnapping. They resort to hiring private armed security guards to surround their houses and accompany them and their children everywhere in public, further increasing their isolation. This heighted militarism and social breakdown already exists in various countries around the world, including right in our neighboring Latin America.

Instead, maintaining a more cohesive society benefits everyone. Even though the wealthy will fight like mad against relinquishing a portion of their wealth in the short-term, doing so will lead to a far better society in the long-term and will thereby improve the lives of all, including the lives of the wealthy.

Another powerful reason exists as well: Happiness.

This conjures the old adage that it is far more rewarding to give than to receive. It turns out that this concept has been verified by research and experimentation. One's own happiness is enhanced by helping others.

This notion has been reflected in diverse cultures throughout the world, including by the Dalai Lama, Mahatma Gandhi, and the Bible. And it has existed throughout time all the way back to ancient civilizations. Our old friend Aristotle even wrote about it in the 4th century B.C., some 2,400 years ago.

According to Aristotle (Politics, Book 7, Part I): "Happiness, whether consisting in pleasure or virtue, or both, is more often found with those who are most highly cultivated in their mind and in their character, and have only a moderate share of external goods, than among those who possess external goods to a useless extent but are deficient in higher qualities."

So even though the wealthy will wail and moan over Mend or Spend, their greater financial contributions to the good of society will no doubt redound to their benefit in the form of their greater happiness in life.

They can thank us later.

Chapter

14

Light-Up the World

Economic inequality plagues not just the United States but many countries around the world. Mend or Spend is the global solution.

Indeed, Mend or Spend knows no bounds and could easily spread to numerous countries and blossom. The advanced democracies in Europe immediately come to mind, such as England, France, Spain, Italy, and Greece. Their electoral systems function with integrity and thus candidates would be free to offer voters the option of Mend or Spend.

Latin America is another area that would benefit greatly from Mend or Spend because it suffers from grievous economic inequality. Countries like Brazil, Colombia, Panama, Chile, and Mexico are examples.

Countries with governments that are more authoritarian and corrupt are environments where Mend or Spend would be less likely to emerge. Russia, China, and various countries in the Middle East and Africa come to mind. Mend or Spend could not be freely offered to the voters in these types of countries. After all, Mend or Spend would pose a dangerous threat to totalitarian regimes. Rumblings along these lines would quickly be suppressed. Any radicals brazen enough to advocate for it would be silenced, jailed, disappeared, or killed.

But all hope is not lost even in strict totalitarian countries. If Mend or Spend were to spread around the world in more democratic nations, then it might just build enough momentum to create an enormous wave that could not be contained. This wave would wash through even the most totalitarian countries as well, cleansing them in its wake.

Chapter

15

Together We Rise

Even though we live in an age plagued with outrageous economic inequality and vast unfairness in society, today, in fact, is a very exciting time to be alive. The reason is that right now We the People have the opportunity to change it.

It seems like the problem is too big. But it's not too big.

It seems like there is no way out of our economic trap. But there is a way out.

It seems like the wealthy are too powerful. But true power is vested in the vote of the people.

America is great because it is a democracy. The common people possess the ultimate power. The wealthy few at the top will constantly seek to suppress the masses down below in order to extract greater and greater wealth for themselves. But the people must resist.

We the People are the masters. Our leaders are our servants.

In our society today, however, the wealthy few at the top have captured the politicians and turned them against the people. The politicians have been reshaping society to benefit the wealthy and suppress the middle class and the poor.

Enough is enough. And we have had enough.

Our past lights the way of our future. We have been here before. Our nation once suffered the scourge of drastic economic inequality during the Gilded Age of the late 1800s and early 1900s. We the People came together, united as one, and lifted ourselves out of the oppression during the Progressive Era in the early part of the 1900s.

We did it before. We can do it again.

We possess the power. Now it us up to us to use it.

History is calling. The need is overwhelming. The opportunity is before us.

We can change the system. We can overcome economic inequality. We can make our society more free and fair for everyone.

But will we do it? Will we unite together? Will we act?

The answer depends entirely upon one person.

You.

Index

www.ingramcontent.com/pod-product-compliance
Lightning Source LLC
Chambersburg PA
CBHW060030210326
41520CB00009B/1073